Charlie's Girl

*Growing up on a Small Nebraska Farm
in the '40s and '50s*

Marje (Smith) Perkins

In loving memory of my parents,
Eva and Charlie Smith.

To my family:

My loving husband, Bob;

My wonderful children;

My brothers and sisters.

Contents

I Remember

Inever appreciated what a deep impression my parents, Charlie and Eva Smith, made on the small farming community where I was raised. Visiting the town of Cambridge to research this book half a century later, I described where I had lived, just outside of town, when several local citizens exclaimed, "Oh, you're Charlie's girl." Mom and dad were a team, and they had four girls, (as well as four boys.) I was glad people remembered us. I was proud to be remembered as "Charlie's girl."

Memories are the blueprint for our identity. They never leave us, they become part of us. Memories are not only the past, but part of the future. So much of who we are today is where we have been in the past.

There are so many things that bring back memories. A simple odor can awaken vivid memories; the smell of fresh baked bread or the refreshing smell of newly mowed hay. An image of an object or place can bring back a moment in time that was pleasant; seeing a smiling grandmother, looking at an old photo, or visiting my hometown. Sounds can trigger a long-ago memory. Music can stir powerful emotions and transport us back in time. The sounds of crickets or coyotes in the distance take me back to my time on the farm. I saw beautiful Hollyhocks in Taos, New Mexico, and suddenly remembered making flower dolls. While eating an oatmeal cookie one day, I recalled milk and cookies with Mrs. Brown. Riding in the car with my granddaughter, prompted me to begin playing the alphabet game.

Family is where life begins and our memories are made. We do not remember whole days; we remember moments. The shared moments become tomorrow memories. Though I have moved on with my life, the memories linger. I love those random memories that make me smile even today.

Friends and places may change, but the memories will last forever.

There's a lot I remember as I look back on those years. I can see it now as if it happened yesterday: the hustle and bustle of a working farm that I saw and felt each day, animals congregated in pens, crops waiting to be harvested, the first snow of winter, Christmas with my family, Saturday night in town, playing kid games around the farm, being teased by my older brothers, anticipating the start of school, the excitement of high school, and leaving for college.

Not being a morning person, I remember opening my eyes and gazing at the sun coming through the window. I preferred pulling the covers over my head and going back to sleep, but morning on the farm begins. The roosters announced morning by stretching their necks and loudly crowing. I hear the cattle in the pens bellowing because it was milking time. I am still lounging in bed as I hear my dad bringing the milk to the basement and my mom rattling pans in the kitchen preparing breakfast. I jump out of bed and get dressed. My dad's jaunty whistling and smile cheer me up as I begin my morning chore of washing the milking machines.

The farm is a contrast of sights, smells, noises, and activities.

I did not like the pungent odors on the farm. I remember how greedy the pigs looked, sounded, and stunk as they squealed and butted each other to be the first at the feeding trough. I watched them gobble their slop. The name for their food even sounds offensive. After a rain, the cattle pens and pig sties gave off a foul smell. I held my nose and wished I could escape to town at that moment.

Chickens and I have a love/hate relationship. I love fried chicken, but I hated taking care of chickens on the farm. I recall going around or through groups of chickens scratching and cackling as they ate their feed and trying to avoid their excrement. I have too many memories of stepping in chicken poop and trying to get the stinking mess off my shoes or bare feet.

The tractor starting in the morning was a sound I liked. The John Deere tractor made a distinctive loud pop, pop, pop. The popping started slow and gradually gained in speed. It was a happy sound that I can still hear in my head.

The quiet and serene sounds and sights of the farm are pleasant recollections. I see pictures in my mind of a glistening field of ripened wheat gently swaying in the breeze, a spectacular sunset lighting up the whole sky and radiating with yellows and oranges, the beautiful night sky with no city lights to dim the bright stars. I can hear the wind quietly blowing through the trees, the tranquility of the windmill pumping water and squeaking as it turns slowly in the wind. The sounds and sights are enjoyable memories because they made me feel peaceful and safe.

The distant howl of coyotes at night was an eerie and frightening sound. I remember feeling a chill hearing them howling.

There was always a yummy aroma coming from the kitchen on the farm: bacon frying, chicken frying, bread baking, cakes baking, pies sitting fresh out of the oven. I can close my eyes and see my mother bending over, opening the oven door, and taking out a beautifully browned pan of bread. I feel nostalgic, like smiling on the inside, when I smell fresh baked bread.

As a child, I loved playing on the farm because there were so many places to explore. I remember swinging in a tire swing hearing the grinding of the rope as the swing shifted back and forth. I remember my brother, Bob, teasing me as I was swinging back and forth on the noisy front gate. He called me Little Lulu. My middle name is Lou and I had long curls. Hiding and playing in the hayloft with friends was a favorite game. Down the hill on the farm was called over the hill. Over the hill was covered with trees, old machinery, and discarded household objects. I remember it as a mysterious playground.

Of course, as a normal teen, I was bored with all the farm endeavors and wanted to live in town. I envisioned my friends in town having all the fun. My friends from Cambridge were thrilled to visit the farm, because they were bored with the confinement of town. Teenagers.

Sunday memories are pleasant. I spent the day with aunts, uncles, and cousins. Sunday was a day to take it easy. In the summer, I remember helping make homemade ice cream. I can hear Mom and Dad laughing and chatting with relatives and friends.

I was born into this bountiful collection of sights, sounds, and smells. I shared it with seven energetic, fun-filled, and inquisitive siblings plus my hardworking and supportive parents.

My regret about my childhood is, I wish I had been more curious about the world beyond Cambridge, Nebraska. All the information that is now available at the touch of a finger was in books, encyclopedias, and newspapers. I wish I had discussed world events with my parents and expanded my horizons.

I remember the simplicity, innocence, hard work, and excitement of growing up on the Smith farm.

Family is where my story begins.

My Family

Wonderful People Who Made Farm Life Vivid

I was born between the Great Depression and America's entry in World War II, into a large farm family at Cambridge, Nebraska.

Marjorie Lou Smith.

Cambridge is a small town in the south-central part of the state. I lived on a farm south and east of Cambridge the first eighteen years of my life. I was born in 1940 at Mrs. Tomlin's Nursing Center in Cambridge. I was the seventh child in a family of eight children, four boys and four girls. It was Labor Day weekend. Later in life I heard my mother say about my birth, "At least I did not have to fry chicken for the Labor Day picnic! Aunt Isabelle wanted to name you Marsha."

My family called me Margie, Margie Lou, or Marjorie. My brother, Bob, dubbed me Little Lulu. "Marge's Little Lulu" was a popular comic

strip character at the time. You notice that my name was spelled with a "g." When I was in high school, I read in a fan magazine that some movie star spelled Marge with a "j." I thought it looked cool and decided to spell my nickname with a "j." I stuck with it and have been correcting people all of my adult life that my name is spelled "Marje." My family members revert to old times and call me Margie or Margie Lou. I remember many times as a child hearing my dad name all of my older sisters before calling my name. I was

*Brother **Norris**, **Marjorie**, and sister **Carole** Ann by the farmyard light pole.*

"Joyce … Joan … MARGIE."

Some notes about my birth year, 1940:

–Franklin Roosevelt was president, 1933-1945.

–Frank Sinatra made his singing debut.

–The first modern freeway opened in Pasadena, California.

–The first successful helicopter flight was made in the U.S.

–And the first McDonalds opened in San Bernardino, California. Good Year!!!! Also in 1940 World War II was raging in Europe, Paris had fallen, and the Blitz had started in England. Not good!!!!

Charles Francis Smith, my father, was born in 1900 at Kenesaw, Nebraska. He moved with his parents to a farm southeast of Cambridge in 1909. He attended Sunny Hillside School and Curtis Agricultural School. Quoting from my Grandmother Perdue's journal, "Charlie was a hard worker and they raised all those children and put them through school and made wise investments all through those years when money was hard to come by." I remember my father as being affable, strong, gentle, and a bit of a tease. If you were attempting to get his permission for something, *maybe* was a clue you might get it, but when he said NO, that was the end of it, and no amount of bargaining, pleading, or begging would change his mind. My father was friendly and would strike up a conversation with total strangers. Looking back, I realize he was partial to his daughters. You could tell that he loved my mother, not that I saw them kiss or hold hands; he appreciated her and treated her with respect and dignity.

Charles Smith.

The earliest memories I have of my father are:

–He always wore overalls.

–Watching him put on his denim jacket and going outside to do chores.

–Always being busy on the farm.

–Hearing him whistle a cheery tune.

–Enjoying a cigar on Saturday.

–Putting on his suit for church on Sunday.

–Making ice cream for Sunday company.

–Laughing and teasing.

–Keeping the furnace supplied with wood and coal in the winter.

–Delivering milk to the grocery stores.

My sister, Joan, gave me an insight into my father's character. Dad was always disappointed that he did not graduate from high school. His older brother and sister graduated. Dad was attending high school at Curtis Agricultural School when his father insisted he quit, come home, and help on the farm. Perhaps this is the reason my dad was so eager for us to graduate from high school and encouraged us to attend college.

I also remember a dessert that my dad would have. He would crumble saltine crackers into a bowl and top them with sugar and milk. I tried it as a kid and thought it was very good. Then one day as an adult I thought of the saltine dessert and tried it. It tasted terrible. Why did I think it was so great as a child?

Family and friends called my father Charlie. A couple of stories I heard about my father are:

–After having three sons he wanted a daughter, then … he got twin daughters. He was quoted as saying, "I guess I prayed a little too hard."

–Another story is about how we stayed in a motel in Colorado. My dad went to the office to pay the bill, and there was a large sign reading, "We do not accept counter checks." (A counter check is a blank check with only the bank name on it, no name or account number.) My dad looked at the owner and said, "You'll take *my* check, won't you? I am good for it." The man looked at my dad's honest face and responded, "Sure."

Every kid and grandchild that went out the door at the farmhouse heard my father yell, "Shut the door, Richard." Who was Richard? No one in our family was named Richard. It became a family tradition. My children still chant the phrase, "Shut the door, Richard." Another well-remembered saying of my father was, "What you don't have in your head, you have to have in your heels." Meaning, plan ahead.

When my father came into the world, happenings in 1900-1903 included:

–William McKinley was elected president of the U.S., defeating Willian Jennings Bryan of Nebraska.

–The Paris World's Fair opened.

–The first zeppelin flight was made in Germany.

–Marconi sent the first wireless transcontinental transmission.

–President McKinley was shot.

–The first Nobel Peace Prize was awarded.

–The Commonwealth of Australia was created.

–And the first Crayola Crayons were produced. In 1908 the Model T Ford was produced and sold.

My mother, Eva Marie (Perdue) Smith, was born in 1904 at Cambridge. When she was 4 years old, the family moved back to my

Eva Marie Perdue, left, and her brother, Clark.

Eva Marie Perdue.

grandmother's home place at Elk Creek, Nebraska, for two years and then returned to Cambridge. Mom was the oldest in a family of four children. She graduated from Cambridge High School in 1922. After high school, she pursued a County Teaching Certificate. Quoting from Grandmother Perdue's journal, "She (my mother) was a good student and took a teacher's course and then could teach school when through. She taught at the rural school just north of town for two years, then one year at the Mousel School north of town. She drove to school and had a car so hard to start. Joe (Grandpa Perdue) would get it started for her each morning and then get the rest off for their school. Joe would take Eva to school affairs at night." My mother met my father at one of those school night functions.

My mother was a very patient woman and seldom raised her voice in anger. The song from "Beaches" composed by Jeff Silber and Larry Henley, "Wind Beneath My Wings," describes my mother's personality. She was always supportive, but not necessarily wanting the attention.

My mother was rather shy but was always there with a helping hand and support. She had a strong impact on people in a quiet, gentle way. My sister-in-law, Norma, suggested "Wind Beneath my Wings" as a song for my mother's funeral. That song still brings tears to my eyes.

The earliest memories I have of my mother are:

–Cooking oatmeal for me and Cream of Wheat for my sister.

–Filling the galvanized tub with warm water for our Saturday night baths.

–She and I listening (on the radio) to the count-down on "Your Hit Parade," so we could tell my older sisters the top songs on the chart for the week.

–Always being there.

–Hanging laundry on the clothesline.

–Curling my hair by wrapping it around metal curlers.

–Making school lunches.

–Making me chocolate sandwiches.

–Making casseroles and cakes to take to the church.

Eva Marie Purdue.

–Working in the Methodist Church kitchen.

–Sewing on her Singer sewing machine.

–Canning fruits and vegetables.

–Preparing food for picnics.

Eva Marie Perdue with
a group of teachers.

–And, cooking for harvesters.

What can I say about my mother? I had the greatest mother a girl could have. She made our home a happy place to grow up. Though she did not overtly show her affection, you knew that she loved you and wanted only the best for you. She always had a happy smile as she did her countless chores, and she always had time for me.

Mom let me enjoy being a kid and a teenager. She did not expect me to cook, clean, sew, and prepare to become a housewife. She did the cooking and sewing while I was busy with all of my school and church activities. I did do

Eva Marie Perdue and friends.
Eva is fifth from left in back row.

household chores and farm chores, and I helped with the family dairy business because I was part of the family. I did the chores because it was expected. Not saying I loved the chores around the farm, but I lived there, and it was my responsibility to help out around the house and on the farm.

Mom cooked for the family, guests at our home, and numerous church functions. My father would look longingly at a freshly baked pie, cinnamon rolls, or a cake before my mom announced that it was on its way to a church or club function. Poor Dad!

My mother made most of my clothes, and I remember waiting impatiently by the sewing machine for her to sew the last stitch so I could wear the new outfit.

The only time I saw my mother get angry was when she once had laryngitis. I sort of ignored her, so she pounded on the wall to get my attention because there were some chores she wanted me to do.

My mother was born before women had the right to vote. The 19th Amendment, giving women the right to vote, became part of the Constitution on August 26, 1920. Women's Suffrage was a long-fought battle in the state of Nebraska. It was eventually settled by the Federal Amendment allowing women to vote. A quote from Nebraskastudies.org 1900-24 observed, "Nebraska was one of the last

Eva on the right and friend.

states west of the Mississippi River to grant women the right to vote. It is difficult to discuss women's suffrage movement in Nebraska without also discussing the prohibition movement. The two debates are joined together like Siamese twins. Opponents of women's suffrage movement were convinced if women received the right to vote, prohibition would become the law."

Though a neighboring state, Wyoming, had given the right for women to vote in 1869, the State of Nebraska did not ratify the 19th Amendment giving women the right to vote until 1917.

My mother did not work outside the home for pay, but she did the cooking, baking, sewing, washing, ironing, cleaning, canning, shopping, and uncounted other jobs dealing with raising a large family on a farm. If she had been paid for the many hours that

Eva and Charles courting.

she spent volunteering at the Cambridge Methodist Church, she would have been quite wealthy.

My mother's teaching certificate.

*Eva and Charles'
wedding picture.*

Notable events the year Mother was born, 1904, included:

–The ice cream cone was created during the St. Louis World Fair.

–Wilber Wright made his first plane flight.

–The New York City subway opened.

–The first New Year's Eve celebration was held in Times Square.

–St. Louis Police tried a new investigation method, fingerprints.

–And Theodore Roosevelt was elected President.

Charles F. Smith and Eva Marie Perdue were married in 1925 at Norton, Kansas. Grace Hampson, my father's sister, and her husband accompanied the couple to Norton. They had a supper reception at Grandpa and Grandma Perdue's house in the evening. Their marriage was a long and happy one. They raised eight children and had 22 grandchildren. My father died

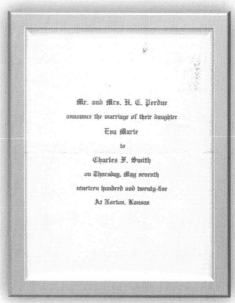

My parents wedding announcement.

15

in 1979, three days before their 54th wedding anniversary. My mother died Feb. 14, 1992. They are both buried in the Cambridge Cemetery.

The only time I heard harsh words between my parents was when they were working on their income taxes. Piles of papers were spread out on the dining room table. Mom and Dad, pencils in hand, were adding up columns of

Mom and Dad on the farm.

numbers. Then I would hear my dad say, "Eva where is that ...?" You just knew to steer clear of the dining room table during income tax time.

We did not have a lot of rules at our house; my parents trusted and

expected their children to make the right choices. We did not want to disappoint our parents. My parents

*Eva and **Charlie** on the farm.*

25th Wedding Anniversary.

16

encouraged us to go out into the world and gave us the opportunity to attend college.

*My brother, **Bob Smith**, served in the Navy during World War II.*

I feel my mom and dad had an enduring influence on my life by giving me the opportunity to grow up happy and well adjusted. My parents set an example for me by the way they lived their lives. They taught me responsibility by being responsible. They taught me love by loving me. They taught me respect by being respectful. They taught me honesty by being honest. They taught me trust by being trustworthy. And they taught me forgiveness because they forgave.

*Margie, in back, **Carole Ann**, left, and Judy Johnson, in our wedding dresses for Bob and Norma's wedding in 1947.*

I have a deep sense of gratitude and appreciation for my parents, who gave so much of themselves for their community and family.

I was blessed with seven brothers and sisters. My brother, Robert (Bob) Darrel Smith, was born at home in 1926 and died in 2013. Bob was inducted into the Navy on his 18th birthday in 1944 and served during the remainder of World War II. He served on the USS Oakland and was in the Pacific and Asiatic Theatres. He returned

*Taking part in Duane and Hazel's marriage in 1952. Back row: **Margie, Norris;** front row: **Carole**, Rusty (Hazel's cousin.)*

home to Cambridge to begin farming after the war. He married Norma Johnson in 1947.

My brother, Paul Dean (Bud) Smith, in 1945.

My brother, Bob, was a tease and somewhat mischievous. The story I have heard about Bob as a young boy is the "tomato incident." Grandma Perdue had a large group of tomatoes picked and laying in her front yard to fully ripen. Bob was warned to stay out of the tomatoes. Upon hearing the warning, he stepped back a few steps and took off running right through the ripening tomatoes, squashing tomatoes with every step. I never heard about the consequences.

My sister, Carole, and I were in Bob and Norma's wedding. My mother made our dresses for the event. After they were married, Bob and Norma moved into an apartment in Grandma Perdue's house.

Paul Dean (Bud) Smith was born in 1927 and died in 2016. Bud got his nickname "Bud," because my parents referred to him as his older brother Bob's "little buddy." Bud graduated from Cambridge High school in 1945 and enlisted in the   Army the same year. He did not serve overseas because World War II was almost over.   Bud was stationed in Arkansas, Kentucky, South Carolina and Washington. He served as an MP at the end of his service. Bud was rather reserved and quiet. My favorite memory of Bud is that he sent me a box of Dentyne Gum while he was in the Army. I was so thrilled to get my very own package in the mail. I kept the box of gum in the kitchen cupboard and sold packs of gum to my brother, Duane, for a nickel.

Bud married Phyllis Downey in 1952. They were married in the Catholic Church. Being raised as a Methodist, I was unfamiliar with the ceremonies and all the statues in the Catholic Church. I was impressed with the elaborate altar. I did not understand the Mass because much of it was in Latin. I remember wearing a hat to their wedding, because it was in the Catholic Church. I had never been in the Catholic Church, and it was an experience for a 12-year-old Methodist kid.

Charles Duane Smith was born in 1930. He was called Duane, his middle name, because he had the same name as my father, Charles. Duane was the first child in the Smith family to attend college.

Duane and Paul Johnson.

Following his graduation from the University of Nebraska in 1952 with a degree in Civil Engineering, Duane enlisted in the Air Force. He joined during the Korean War. Because of his college degree he was given a commission as a 2nd lieutenant. Duane took his basic training at Lackland Air Force Base in San Antonio, Texas. He was stationed at Keesler Air Force Base at Biloxi, Mississippi, and attended Radar School. Duane bought Carole and me sombreros when he was stationed in Biloxi.

Duane married his high school sweetheart, Hazel Edgerton, in June

*Joan, **Margie Lou**, Joyce.*

of 1952. Hazel was at our house quite often on Sundays. On one Sunday visit, Duane took Hazel for a ride on our horse, Beauty. He intentionally kicked the horse in the flanks which caused Beauty to begin bucking. We all thought it was SO funny. Not sure if he wanted to scare Hazel or just make her hang onto him tighter?

At Duane and Hazel's wedding, I remember walking down the aisle with my brother, Norris, before the ceremony to light the candelabras. I had trouble lighting one of the candles, and I was so nervous because it was taking so long. As candle lighters, Norris and I wore white choir robes. I did not get to wear a fancy dress like my little sister, Carole. She was a flower girl in the wedding. Another cute wedding dress for Carole.

The first girls in the Smith family were twins. Joyce Marie and Joan Mae Smith were born in 1932. Joyce was born at 5:30 a.m. and Joan was born 10 minutes later at 5:40 a.m. Joyce passed away in 2008. Being twins, they received a lot of attention in the family. My father insisted that they dress alike. Rather than use their individual

Joan and *Joyce*, *the twins.*

names, frequently Joyce and Joan were called "The Twins." The local paper wrote an article about Joyce

Left to right: **Norris, Margie, Carole.**

Joyce, Carole, Joan.

and Joan's 1949 graduation from Cambridge High School. The Cambridge Clarion reported, "Charlie Smith's twins were respectively named valedictorian and salutatorian." I ask you: Did my mother not

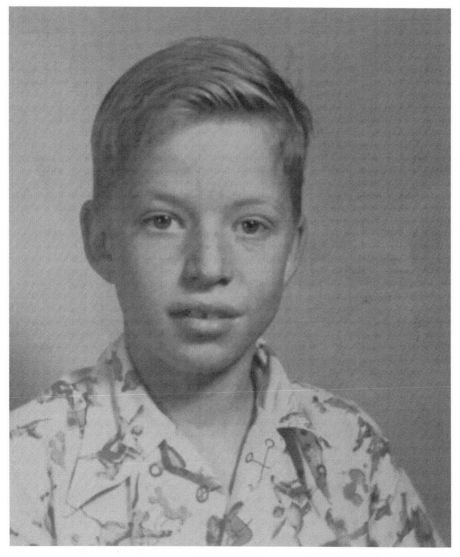

Norris Smith.

deserve equal credit for the twins? I have to realize that it was a small town, the year was 1949, and a man was the head of the family.

Joan was a tomboy and loved being outside on the farm. Joan was also very artistic. Joyce was more refined, helped mom around the house, and played the piano.

When I was in third grade, my sisters were my ride to and from school. I remember hearing a story about one of their after-school escapades. The twins and some friends were driving around after school. While driving over the railroad tracks, the car stalled. The girls were all in a panic; they heard a train coming! Everyone piled out of the car and franticly pushed and pushed until they successfully got the car off the tracks.

When we four sisters started taking our Smith Sister trips in 1982, Joyce and Joan became good friends as well as sisters. While sister-tripping, we went to Hawaii, Virginia, California, Iowa, and Georgia.

Norris, Carole, and I were what was referred to as the second family. There is a seven-year gap between the arrival of the twins and Norris's birth. I am sure my parents thought their family was complete after Joyce and Joan were born. Norris Max Smith was born in 1939 at Grandma and Grandpa Perdue's house in Cambridge. Norris had a very distinctive name and did not have a nickname. Norris was a year and a half older than me and was a great older brother.

Norris got his learner's permit at age 14 and drove us – Carole, himself and me – to and from school. According to Norris, he drove the old green pickup, and on the way to school we delivered milk to customers in Cambridge.

*Joyce, Bonnie (holding **Norris**,) **Joan**.*

Left to right: Cousin Sarah Jane Irwin, **Carole Ann**.

My brother, Norris, has a great story of my father being quite frugal. When Dad purchased the green pickup, a heater for the pickup was an optional feature. We lived in Nebraska which gets very cold in the winter, but my father decided not to spend the extra money on a heater for the green pick-up. Norris remembers constantly scraping ice from the windshield in order to see where he was going. We had to ride with the windows down so our breath would not cause more frost on the windshield as we were going to and from school.

Norris would get very irritated because he had to wait on me to get ready for school *every* morning. I heard him ask my mother what seemed like a thousand times, "Can I just LEAVE her?"

After graduating from high school, Norris bought a great used car. It was a maroon and white two-door hardtop Willys Aero Eagle. My sister-in-law, Marie, joked that Norris could park his cool car in front of John's Drug Store and attract all the cute girls in town. I remember Norris driving me to school activities in his Willys.

Norris served six months in the National Guard after high school.

Carole *and* **Margie** *with their sombreros.*

25

Carole Ann in another wedding, of Bud and Phyllis in 1952.

He went to Ft. Leonard Wood, Missouri, for basic training. I remember getting letters from one of Norris's buddies in the National Guard. His buddy came for a visit after they finished their training. I thought he was very handsome and I tended to hang around while Norris's friend was visiting.

My little sister, Carole Ann, the baby of the family, was born in 1945. Carole was the only one of the children born in the hospital. "Curly Ann" was Carole's nickname. (Cute when you are little, but how embarrassing around your friends.)

Carole and I fixed up a basement room into a sort of nightclub/playhouse, and we pretended that we were dancers. Carole had gotten a record player for Christmas and we had a few 45 rpm records. Our favorite song to sing and dance to was "Jambalaya" by Hank Williams. We asked our dad and mom to come downstairs and watch our *show,* then we served Mom and Dad a snack as they sat on the floor at our table.

Curly Ann (Carole) on her tricycle.

Because Carole is the baby of the family, we all tease her about being spoiled. She was in seventh grade when I went to college, so she was like an only child. Carole Ann actually kept Mom and Dad young. She was instrumental in persuading my parents to take a trip to Europe in 1965. She continues to be the cement that holds our family together and is the go-to person for family communications.

1953 Family Photo
Back row, left to right, Glenn Moore, Della Deterding (Dad's sister), **Bob***, Phyllis Smith,*
Dad*; next row, Dorothy Moore,* **Mom***, Grandma Perdue, Norma Smith holding Roger,*
Bud*, Hazel, Larry Moore; next row,* **Norris** *(hiding),* **Joan, Joyce, Marjorie***, Dick Moore;*
front row, Glenda Moore, **Carole Ann,** *and Mike Smith.*
Photo taken by my brother, Duane.

*1952 – Smith Family, left to right: back row, **Duane and Hazel, Phyllis and Bud, Bob and Norma**; middle row, **Joyce, Dad, Mom, Joan**; front row, **Norris, Carole**, holding nephew **Roger**, **Margie** holding nephew **Mike**.*

*This is another picture of my mother, **Eva Marie Perdue**, and her brother, Clark.*

The Place I Called Home

Growing With the Family and Changing With the Times

I lived on a farm one-half mile south and about three miles east of Cambridge. That was my home until I left to attend college in Lincoln in 1958. I had one address as a kid – "Cambridge, Nebr." There was no street address, zip code, box number, or a house number. My mail came to: "Marjorie Smith, Cambridge, Nebr." Amazing!

In 1935 the Smith Farm was down by the Republican River. My father called it *bottom land*. A quote from Grandma Perdue's journal, "Eva and Charlie's farm was on the south side of the Republican River and was just about straight south of our house on the north side of the river. The men used to ford the river to go back and forth to help each other farm. The house and farm buildings were underwater in the 1935 Flood."

Though I was not born until 1940, the Republican River Flood of 1935 greatly affected my home, my family, the family farm, and the town of Cambridge. My grandparents, parents, older brothers, and sisters all have memories of the '35 Flood.

Smith farm home.

On Memorial Day in 1935 during the Dust Bowl and a severe drought in the Midwest, a devastating flood along the Republican River caused a tremendous amount of destruction in southwestern Nebraska. A few days earlier there had been torrential rains, the ground was saturated and the streams were full and overflowing. Then, on the night of Memorial Day, Thursday, May 30 in 1935, a deluge of rain measuring nearly 24 inches fell in eastern Colorado and southwest Nebraska. The next morning the usually calm Republican River was filling "bluff to bluff" just as early Native Americans had predicted. The river flowed east from the Colorado border and gained in capacity and intensity. The Republican River created a wall of water as it rolled across southern Nebraska.

It was not a quiet flood. Survivors recalled hearing the water before they could see it. Fed by swollen streams along the way, it was consuming everything in its path. The raging river contained trees, livestock, crops, and pieces of buildings, bridges, railroads, and highways. In places, the floodwater spread two miles on each side of the river banks.

The flood destroyed homes, businesses, highways, railroad lines, and bridges throughout southwest Nebraska and into Kansas. In Cambridge, nearly 70 percent of the buildings was destroyed. Farmland containing crops and hay were ruined. According to the "U.S. Geological Survey," Nebraska losses included 94 people, 8,100 head of livestock, 57,000 acres of farmland, and 307 highway bridges.

Photo courtesy of Cambridge Museum.

My brother, Duane, who was 4 years old at the time, recalls getting up in the morning and seeing the floodwater rising from the river and coming into the house. The family made a hurried exit from the house. They – Mom, Dad, Bob, age 9, Duane, 4, Joyce and Joan, 3 – rode a horse across floodwater to the road where a neighbor with a team of horses hitched to a hayrack picked them up. Duane remembers that one of his sisters lost a shoe in the water while riding to the hayrack. The family rode on the hayrack to a farm owned by my aunt and uncle, Grace and Denny Hampson. With a minimum of provisions, everyone stayed in the *haymow*, hayloft, of the barn. (If you are not from the Midwest, the term haymow rhymes with cow.) They stayed for two days as the water rose and began to flood the Hampson's farm. In addition to all the other problems, the children had chicken pox. My brother, Duane, remembers, after spending the night in the haymow, the next morning the men moved a stove onto a hayrack and cooked eggs for breakfast.

Mom told me they tied a rope around Dad's waist as he waded into the house to retrieve any food that was available. Apparently, there were some eggs, lima beans, and canned sardines among the food collected. My oldest brother, Bob, commented later that he hated lima beans, but he ate them because he was hungry. Yuk on the sardines! Mom said the group in the haymow ate what was available to survive.

I remember my mom's conversation about how the drafty old barn creaked, moaned, and swayed as the floodwater rose around it. The noise of the water lapping against the barn kept them awake most of the night. Everyone prayed that the barn would not collapse.

In the book "Bluff-to-Bluff" by Marlene (Harvey) Wilmont, there is an excerpt of a letter from a woman caught in the 1935 flood. The woman writes that after spending the night in a tree, she waded in water waist deep to Denny Hampson's hayloft for shelter. She noted that Charlie Smith's flock and several others were harbored there.

After two days in the haymow of the barn, my brother, Duane, recalls that he along with Mom, Dad, Bob, Joyce, Joan, Aunt Grace, and Uncle Denny went by boat to the home of Claude and Ada Johnson. The Johnson's house was on higher ground and did not flood. My brother vividly remembers looking back at Grace and Denny's house as they were being rowed away and saw that the flood water had split the roof of the house.

Photo courtesy of Cambridge Museum.

My brother, Bud, age 7, was staying with Grandma and Grandpa Perdue on the other side of the river that week because he did not have chicken pox. Seeing that the Republican River was beginning to flood, Grandma, Grandpa, Bud, and other family members left their house and took refuge at Uncle Clark's house in the hills north of town.

My brother, Duane, heard Mom remark that the water level in their flooded house was one inch below the frying pan sitting on the stove. My sister-in-law, Norma, relayed an incident about my mother's bread dough. The bread was rising in pans when the family hurriedly left the house. When they returned to the house following the flood, the pans of bread were floating on top of floodwater and looked like they were ready to be put in the oven.

Quoting from Grandma's journal: "The flood of 1935 hit them (Mom and Dad) very hard, in fact they were really in it. They spent a couple of nights in a barn at Denny Hampson's.

"The same flood ruined all our land and we lost all we had worked 20 years for. I thought it the worst tragedy that could happen but later realized it wasn't."

After the '35 Flood, my parents purchased another farm and moved their flooded house to higher ground. My brother, Duane, only 4 at the time, tells how the house was jacked up and put on wheels. He explained a very complicated piece of equipment, a capstan, a large pulley with cables, was used to move the house. According to Merriam-Webster Dictionary, a capstan is "a machine that turns so that a rope or cable can wind around it and move or lift heavy weights." My brother remembers the horses walking around the capstan winding the cables to pull the house forward. With each move, the capstan had to be repositioned in front of the house, the cables unwound, and the horses could again wind the cables to move the house. Planks were placed under the wheels because of the muddy ground. The house was moved about one half- mile across muddy fields and up a hill to its new location. With so much information for a four-year old to grasp, it's no wonder Duane became an engineer when he grew up.

My brother, Norris, remembers Dad telling him they also moved the barn and a chicken coop from the farm by the river to the present location.

There was a house on the new farmstead, and the family lived there until the flooded house was moved and cleaned. At a later time, Dad had a basement dug under the house in order to install a furnace. Prior to placing the furnace in the basement, the house was heated with a potbellied stove.

The house as I remember it, was atop a small hill and close to a well-traveled dirt road leading to Cambridge. The house had one bedroom, plus a bedroom added to the south part of the house, and an enclosed porch made into a bedroom. The outside door to the house was located in the porch adjoining the kitchen. There was a living room and a dining room divided with two large wooden doors. The dining room was quite large and provided a place for many other activities besides eating. It was a warm room in the winter because of the floor furnace. The large dining room table was used for a multitude of activities: folding clothes, bookkeeping, studying, playing games, sewing, crafts, etc. The living room doors were usually closed in the winter to keep all the heat in the dining room. Another door from the kitchen opened to the basement stairs. There was also an outside door leading to the basement.

The house had one very large walk-in closet for storage. It contained clothes, mementos, Christmas decorations, sewing supplies, outgrown clothes, and boxes of things that I have no idea what was in them. My little nephew, Mike, was visiting the farm one day. As we were working and talking, we noticed that Mike had wandered off. We began hunting for him. We searched every building on the farm, the basement, and in the trees. After at least an hour of searching, he walked out of the closet, oblivious to our panic. He had fallen asleep under some clothes in the back of that large closet.

The kitchen was the hub of activity because my mom was always cooking and there was a door to the outside. Part of the kitchen was sort of a mud room, and everyone came in that door to take off their boots and coats. Eight kids plus my parents lived in that house. ONE BATHROOM! (Or outhouse when I was very young.)

The house was remodeled many times while I was growing up. Each time a wall was taken down or moved, dried mud from the '35 Flood was found. An indoor bathroom was added. Later the wall between the dining room and living room was removed, making it one large room. During another remodel, the huge walk-in closet was turned into a hallway and storage closets.

Sleeping arrangements were a little tight in our house. My brother, Duane, remembers sleeping with his two brothers in one bed. My parents' bedroom was a remodeled front porch. The boys slept in the basement when we were all at home. I always shared a bedroom with my sister, Carole. When Carole and I were younger, we had the south porch bedroom. When my sisters, Joyce and Joan, moved to Lincoln, Carole and I moved into the real bedroom with a closet for our clothes. My brother, Norris, moved to the south porch bedroom. I always lived in the same house, but it kept changing.

As a baby, my sister, Carole, slept on what the family referred to as "the box." This was a large white wooden storage container for toys, located in my parents' bedroom. I remember the top of the box was covered with a blue vinyl material. In my memory, it was the same material my mother used in re-upholstering our old car. With a blanket added to make it comfortable, the top of "the box" served as a baby bed for Carole.

When grandchildren came to spend the night at the house, my dad would tease them. Dad told the grandkids, "Go to sleep, and we will just hang you on a nail." I noticed a look of confusion and apprehension in their eyes. The grandkids didn't think it was a funny joke. But to their relief, they woke up the next morning still on the couch or the rollaway bed.

We had one telephone in our house, a wooden wall phone, in the kitchen. It had a mouthpiece, a crank to ring the operator, a receiver that you held up to your ear, a hook to hang the receiver on which also disconnected your call, (hence the term "hang up" on a phone call.) There were no dials. You gave a person's telephone number to an operator, and she connected you to the correct phone. The bells on top of the phone rang when you got a phone call. The Smith family phone number was 3F210. Our family had what was called a party line, and each person on the party line had a particular ring indicating a phone call. Our ring was two short rings and one long ring. Other people sharing the line had different rings, and we heard their ring. You could also (*of course, I didn't do this*) listen to other people's phone calls on our line. It was called *rubbering*. One time my mother, not rubbering, picked up the phone to make a call, and a neighbor was already on the line. My mom heard the neighbor lady say, "Yes, the Smiths were over last night for popcorn, and my house is a mess." That comment was used in jest by our family on numerous occasions when we needed to do some cleaning.

Photo courtesy of Arapahoe Museum

The phone was also a source of mass communication. The operator would place what was called an emergency call. The call consisted of several long rings, and everyone on our party line would listen to the call. The calls were more a source of information rather than actual emergencies. The emergency calls I remember were informing everyone that a train car of coal had arrived in town.

One stormy night, lightning struck the telephone line outside the house, and the charge came in through our phone. The force blew the mouthpiece of the phone across the kitchen and melted other parts of the phone.

> Lesson: Do not talk on the phone during a lightning storm!

It made an ear-splitting bang waking up the entire household from a sound sleep.

When I was 13 years old, the television station in Holdrege, Nebraska, began broadcasting. My dad, excited about it, bought a television set two weeks before the station was on the air. The family watched snow on the screen for two weeks. The television station began broadcasting the evening of December 24, 1953. We eagerly watched as they turned on all the switches and began broadcasting. Channel 13 was the first and only television station available in the area. In the beginning, it was only on the air between 7 and 10 at night. A new era began for the Smith family.

The first television show I remember watching was Ed Sullivan on Sunday night. Since our family had one of the few television sets among the neighboring farms, all of our neighbors would pop in to watch Ed Sullivan on Sunday nights. We had chairs and couches lined up in rows to accommodate everyone. (Now people call this their media room.) My mom would be busy in the kitchen fixing snacks for the guests. Ed Sullivan introduced many new musical acts including Elvis Presley and the Beatles.

As Channel 13's broadcast time expanded, I remember coming home after high school and watching "American Bandstand" with Dick Clark. "American Bandstand" was broadcast nationally starting in

1957. I became enthralled with some of the dance couples on the show. The premise of the show was that pop music stars performed and were interviewed by Dick Clark. A group of teenage couples danced to recorded music, and the cameras televised them dancing. Sounds dull, but it was a very popular show. There were regulars on the show, so I began to follow them. You can compare it to "Dancing with the Stars" of today.

My dad loved to watch "Gunsmoke" on Saturday nights. A few other shows I remember watching were "The Dinah Shore Show," "Leave It To Beaver," "Father Knows Best" and "Zorro." TV was not a significant part of my free time as a kid because I was in junior high when television arrived at our home.

When we got our television set, we also had to get a TV antenna which was mounted on the top of the house. Because the TV station was a long distance from our house, the antenna had to be very high and pointed toward the television station transmitter. It would take three people to get the antenna properly adjusted: one person on top of the house adjusting the antenna, another watching the TV set to determine the least snowy picture, and one outside shouting directions to both of the others. Reminds me of getting my eyes checked. Is this better, or is this better? It was a process of fine tuning the direction of the antenna.

When I was a small child, we had a floor furnace in the dining room to keep the whole house warm. Each winter my dad would have coal delivered and emptied into a basement opening (window) above the furnace room. Dad would keep a wood and coal fire going in the big furnace downstairs during the winter. Above the furnace in the dining room was a heavy metal floor grate, and the heat from the furnace came up through the grate. The grate got so hot that you could burn your bare feet if you stood on it. There was no fan to circulate the heat, so the bedrooms were very cold. As a kid in the winter, I would get dressed sitting by the furnace.

A family story about the furnace is the "roasting of my brother-in-law." My sister, Joyce, brought her boyfriend, Ed, home to meet the family, and we entertained him with a big family meal. We put leaves in the dining room table and stretched it the length of the room to seat the whole clan. It was winter, and my dad had the furnace stoked up to the max. About halfway through the dinner, Ed began to turn red, and sweat was running down his face. (On the farm, we called it sweat.) He was so polite that he did not say a word about the heat. His chair was sitting over the floor furnace grate. After numerous apologies, my mother sat Ed in a much cooler place at the table. Not sure we ever convinced Ed we didn't put him "on the hot seat" on purpose. We gave Ed a warm welcome into our family. He married my sister, Joyce, on September 19, 1954.

Later the furnace was replaced by a propane heater. It sat on the north wall of the dining room. I remember hearing the term isinglass when referring to a part of the heater. Not sure what it was, but I kept hearing that strange word in connection with the heater. The brown heater had an orange glow in the front as the heating element came on. A fan circulated heat out the top of the heater. It was very warm in front of the heater. There was a clicking sound as it turned on and off. The brown heater, as was the floor furnace, was the only source of heat for the whole house. I also sat in front of the brown heater and got dressed on cold winter mornings.

Margie and *Carole* celebrating a birthday. *Margie with her curls.*

I fondly remember taking my Saturday night bath in a galvanized tub in the kitchen when I was very young. My mother would heat some water on the stove to make the bathwater warmer. The tub was in the kitchen (there was no bathroom at that time) which was a warm room because of the wood-burning cook stove. I am sure more than one person took a bath in that same tub of water. I remember it as a warm fun time of the week. Baths were on Saturday night as we needed to be clean and dressed up for church on Sunday.

Mom curled my hair by putting metal curlers in my hair. After taking out the curlers, she fixed my hair by combing the curls of hair around her finger. For several years, I had long curls.

Monday on the farm was wash day. In the Midwest, it is pronounced "worsh." My mother probably used a wash board and tub for laundry at one time, but I remember the Maytag wringer washer down in our basement. It was a white machine, round in shape, and had a wringer

Maytag wringer washer.

attachment on top, a black knob on the side, a hose to drain the water, a motor under the round tub, and four legs.

On Monday morning, the laundry chute from the bathroom closet to the basement was stuffed full of dirty clothes waiting to be washed. In the bathroom, the laundry chute was a small cabinet door leading to a hole in the floor. In the basement beside the washer a huge five-foot cloth bag hung from the ceiling under the bathroom clothes chute. Mom made the laundry chute bag by sewing several flour sacks together. The large bag was closed by a string tied around at the bottom of the bag. The laundry chute resembled a punching bag in a gymnasium. I am quite sure the Smith kids punched on the bag as they watched it grow larger and larger as it filled with dirty clothes during the week.

In preparation for wash day, Mom untied the string at the bottom of the bag, sending a huge pile of laundry onto the basement floor. No telling how many little surprises accidently made it into the laundry chute during the week: lost toys, coins, skate keys, tools, etc.

My mother would fill the washing machine with water from a hose and kettles of hot water from the kitchen, add soap, put in a load of wash, pull the black knob on the side of the washer, put the lid on the washer, and the washing began. I was fascinated by the black button because it started the slosh-slosh-slosh noise of the agitator.

After letting the clothes agitate in the washer, Mom would push in the black knob and begin putting the items through the wringer. A wringer is two rollers under spring tension that would literally squeeze the water out of the clothes or linens. The wringer could be dangerous if you were to get your fingers, hand, or hair in it. If you were not careful, the wringer would also break buttons or zippers.

After going through the wringer, the washed clothes were then placed in a galvanized tub full of water to rinse the wash load. The wringer could be rotated to be above either the washer or the rinse tub. The rinsing was done by hand, then the items went through the wringer again. The washed and rinsed clothes went into a laundry basket. The process was repeated for each load of wash. The first load to be washed was whites, then colors, then heavily soiled clothing because the washer was filled only once. With all the washing that had to be done, our family wore our clothes more than one day. My mother washed clothing, sheets, and towels.

After everything was washed, rinsed, and put into laundry baskets, it had to be taken up the stairs and outside to the clothesline in summer and winter. The *worsh* was hung on the clothesline using clothes pins, then left to dry. Just imagine at least four long clotheslines full of drying clothing, sheets, and towels. In warm weather, everything dried in the gentle Nebraska breeze and smelled so fresh. Well, not always a gentle breeze in Nebraska. In the winter, not so ideal, fingers froze while putting the wet laundry on the clothesline. A trick was to put a hot-water bottle in the clothespin bag to warm your fingers.

I seemed to arrive home from school in time to take in the wash, which means unpinning it and bringing it inside. I remember in the winter the sheets and towels were frozen and crackled as you took them down from the line. You could say they were freeze-dried. Everything was also very stiff. Mom did have a few clotheslines in the basement to hang some of the laundry in the winter.

The process was not over yet. The next task was ironing. There was no wash and wear. Clothing was made of cotton, so dresses, shirts, and blouses all had to be ironed. There were no spray bottles or steam irons. Before we had electricity, I am sure my mother had to heat a flat iron on the stove and then iron, but I remember my mother using an electric iron. Items to be ironed had to be dampened. My mother called it sprinkling the clothes. She would dip her hand in water and shake it over the item of clothing and then roll each item up and put it in a basket to stay moist until it was ironed. Instead of ironing jeans and slacks, she used pant stretchers in them. They were wire frames inserted into the trouser legs when wet and pulled out to stretch them, thus eliminating wrinkles. The jeans were dried with the stretchers in them. You can still purchase pant stretchers.

When I was growing up, we did not have a large variety of clothing. We wore the same clothes several days. I always changed into everyday clothes when I came home from school or church. My mother handmade most of my clothing. She had a Singer treadle sewing machine. When not in use (seldom) it folded down to look like a table. It was powered by a foot pedal, treadle, that my mother pushed back and forth with her feet to power the sewing machine.

Mom and I went to the local store, Thorndike's, to purchase items to make clothes. We looked through a pattern book to find a picture of a style resembling the dress, skirt, or blouse I wanted. We gave the clerk the name of the style and size needed. The pattern was an envelope with the picture on the front and thin pattern pieces neatly folded inside. (The Butterick brand was the first to use tissue paper for their patterns.) Next, we picked the material (fabric) which Thorndike's had in bolts. The pattern suggested how many yards needed for a garment. The store also sold thread, snaps, hook-and-eyes, zippers, and buttons.

Fabrics and shoes at Thorndike's, my favorite store. This is the women's part of the store. Those tables of women's shoes appear to show prices of $1.75 and $2.39. Thorndike's was open for 70 years, closing in 1973.

At home, Mom would lay out the pattern pieces on top of the fabric. She weighted the pattern pieces down on the fabric with glasses from the kitchen cupboard. Then Mom cut out the pieces of the garment and sewed them together. Buttons and buttonholes, zippers, snaps, and trim were all added. Remarkable ... I had a new skirt, dress, or blouse.

Sometimes Mom and I went to Penney's in McCook (a much larger town than Cambridge) for the items. She ordered some clothes from the Sears and Roebuck catalog. When I was younger, my mother made the decisions about the clothes I needed. I am sure there were many hand-me-downs, dresses made from flour and feed sacks, or blouses made from left-over fabric. (Manufacturers sold flour and animal feed in cotton printed bags.) My mother was a good seamstress, and I liked the clothes she made. Mom would make Easter dresses for my sister and me. Occasionally we got new shoes and hats as well.

I have fond memories of a number of items that were always in our house. A picture of *Old Ironsides*, green and dark, was always hanging on the wall in the living room. Another item was a silver candy dish that sat prominently on the buffet. It usually had odds and ends of junk in it, not candy. I speculate that the candy dish was a gift on Mom and Dad's 25th wedding anniversary (silver). The silver (tin) cake cover was

very prominent in our house. My mother took it filled with delicious cakes to bake sales, club meetings, and church dinners. Occasionally there was a cake for the family. My dad longed for the day that one of the cakes would not go out the door. I am fortunate to have these items and the memories that they evoke.

My mother's cake cover.

The Smith Family's Sleepy Eye syrup pitcher.

All the Smith kids remember the *syrup pitcher*. Mom would make a very thin, but delicious syrup. Mom's syrup was so tasty on her great pancakes. After preparing the syrup on the stove, she would pour the syrup into the blue-and-white pitcher. When not full of homemade syrup, the pitcher sat prominently on the kitchen counter.

The pitcher was a Sleepy Eye Pattern and manufactured by Monmouth Western Stoneware Company. The Sleepy Eye pieces were used as premiums and promotional items by the Sleepy Eye Milling Company of Sleepy Eye, Minnesota. The blue-and-white series was made from 1906 through 1936. I am guessing that Mom got the pitcher as a premium when buying the many bags of flour that she used feeding a large family. My niece now has the syrup pitcher sitting prominently on a shelf in her dining area.

Sitting in a niche in the Smith family kitchen was a 1940's vintage Porcelier teapot decorated with sailboats. When Mom made herself a cup of tea, she used the sailboat teapot. She made her tea with Lipton loose tea, no tea bags or pods, for her occasional cup of tea. I broke the teapot transporting it to

Porcelier teapot with sailboats.

California. After I carefully glued it together, it now sits on my bookshelf. As I gaze at the teapot decorated with sailboats, I have a warm feeling and a picture of my mother relaxing with her cup of tea. I am disappointed with myself that I did not inquire about the history of the keepsakes.

Above the sink in the kitchen was an old picture, green in color, called *Girl on a Bench*. As I was washing dishes, I used to stare at it and wonder who she was and what was her story. I found a similar picture, or a copy, in an antique store and bought it. Looking at the picture takes me back to standing quietly in the farmhouse kitchen. Now in my travels, I take photos of benches.

The rollaway bed brings to mind another fond memory. The rollaway was a bed that folded up and rolled into the closet when not in use. The bed was in the large walk-in closet sitting under hanging clothes with a quilt draped over it. Later during a remodeling project, a special closet was designed for the rollaway bed. The rollaway bed was for visiting guests, but I remember sleeping on it with my sister, Carole. I surmise the rule was, if the guests were older than my sister and I, they got our bedroom, and we got the rollaway bed.

My dad received a Lava Lamp as a gift for serving on the Board of Directors of the Cambridge Co-op. I was not living at home when he received the lamp, but I know that lava lamp entertained all the grandchildren. (A note about the lava lamp. It was invented by a British accountant in 1963 after watching a homemade egg timer, which was made from a cocktail shaker, as it was bubbling on a stove in a pub.)

The Smith Farm

Making the Most of Every Opportunity

My father was a farmer who was continuously exploring opportunities to grow and improve the Smith family farm. Dad raised a variety of livestock: cattle, pigs, sheep, and chickens. A variety of crops grew on the farm: corn, wheat, cane, alfalfa, and watermelon. Dad also operated a small dairy. He sold milk to two

Barn at the Smith farm.

grocery stores, the creamery, and restaurants in Cambridge. (This was when one could sell what was called raw milk.) The dairy was a family operation. Running the dairy was a seven-days-a-week, 365-days-a-year job. I remember my dad using two Surge electric milking machines for milking the dairy cows. Norris, who was 4 years old at the time, remembers that Dad bought the electric milking machines in 1943. The electric milking machines were powered by

My nephew, Roger, son of my brother, Bob, sits on our electric milking machines — Surge Bucket Milkers – used in the Smith dairy operation.

a generator before electricity was available on the farm in 1945. The cows had to be milked each morning and evening. If we left for the day, we always had to be home around five o'clock to milk the cows and bottle the milk. My father referred to this as *doing the chores*. On the rare occasion that my father was not there, one of my older brothers stepped in and did the chores.

Around five o'clock in the afternoon, the milk cows were brought up from the pasture and herded into the milking barn. My father or the boys in the family milked the cows, using the electric

Curly Ann *– my sister, Carole — sitting on the fence of the milk barn with brother **Duane**.*

milking machines. My younger sister, Carole, said she helped with the milking after all the brothers and sisters had left the farm. Even though I was born and raised on a farm, I do not know how to milk a cow! The girls' jobs were to wash the bottles, the milking machines, and the milk separator. My mother would call the two grocery stores each evening to see how many quarts of milk they needed the following day. My dad knew how many bottles of milk to prepare.

My father carried the milk from the barn to the basement of the house in tall milk cans. The milking machines also had to be brought to the basement to be washed. After carrying the milk from the barn, my dad would fill bottles with milk and place them in a tank of cold water to keep them cool until morning. He also ran some of the milk through the separator so that he could sell the cream. The "swill" (skim milk) was fed to the pigs. (A separator is a centrifugal machine that separates milk into cream and skimmed milk.)

In the mornings, the milk bottles were loaded into milk carriers. Dad loaded the milk carriers into the car and he, or the kids on their way to school, delivered the milk to the grocery stores. In the late

Separator, used to separate milk and cream. Photo courtesy of Arapahoe Museum.

afternoon, on our way home from school, the empty bottles were picked up from the stores and brought home. That was an old-fashioned dairy operation. Instead of getting paid at the grocery stores, our family took it out in trade. Every month, my dad would go to the grocery stores to *settle up*; Dad had to write a check if we bought too much at the store or get some money back if we didn't spend as much.

According to my brother, Norris, he vividly remembers that Dad quit selling milk to the grocery stores in 1957. This was the year Norris graduated from high school. According to Norris, Dad did not think we girls, Carole and I, could deliver the milk. I think the reason Dad quit selling milk was that in 1957 pasteurized milk was preferable to raw milk. Changing times at the Smith Farm.

I have a hazy recollection of sheep on the Smith farm when I was quite young. I remember they were in a pen south of the barn and housed in what was later the milking barn. My brother, Duane, confirmed that we did indeed have a flock of about 100 sheep on the farm. He told me about his chore of herding the sheep to and from the pasture. Duane said sheep were very difficult to herd, but if he could get one of the sheep headed in the right direction, the rest of the flock would follow. He remembers getting off the horse numerous times to get them going. To protect sheep from wild, roaming coyotes, they were brought back up to the barn every evening.

In the spring, Dad would shear the sheep and sell the wool. Duane remembers monster-sized burlap bags holding all the wool from the sheep. In addition to the wool, Dad sold many of the lambs. Duane recalls having a lamb as a 4H project. He felt bad when he had to sell his 4H sheep.

The shearing of the sheep stands out in my memory. I remember how pretty and soft the sheep were, standing in the pen. Then, I recall how the sheep looked and sounded after the shearing. They looked raggedy, like after a terrible haircut. And, they came out the barn door bleating so loud that everyone on the farm heard them. I felt sorry for the poor shabby-looking sheep. I was told shearing did not hurt, it was like getting a haircut. My brother, Duane, gave me a more plausible explanation. Because of the large amount of sheep, they were sheared very quickly, not neatly. Dad was using razor-sharp shears and some sheep were nicked during their shearing.

Duane also tells about a very aggressive ram butting my sister, Joan, when she walked into the sheep pen. Duane admitted that he, Bob, and Bud may have been teasing that old ram.

Raising sheep was another example of how my father diversified his farm to support our family.

Corn was the main crop on the Smith Farm. Corn was sold as a cash crop and also used for feeding the cattle. Some of the corn stalks were

Marjorie eating watermelon on an old-fashioned corn picker.

used to make silage to feed cattle in the winter. In the spring, my father prepared the fields for the corn crop. He used a number of farm implements to get the ground ready for a new corn crop. A disk was used to till the soil and to break up any weeds or corn stalks from last year's corn crop. The plow broke, turned, and mixed the soil. A harrow broke up and smoothed the ground. When the field was cleared, turned, mixed, and smoothed, a lister was used to plant the corn. A lister makes ridges and furrows (long trenches) in the field. The lister my dad used had two round canisters that stored and dropped seeds at intervals into the furrows while another attachment covered the seeds, two rows of corn at a time.

On one occasion, I remember helping my dad by riding on the seat of the lister which Dad pulled with a tractor. I helped by pulling a long lever on the lister at the end of each row, as my father turned the tractor and lister around and started two new rows. The lister was disengaged so it would not plow or plant corn in the road at the end of the field.

In the summer, the field was cultivated and hoed to eliminate the weeds. In the days before irrigation and special fertilizers, a good corn crop was "knee high by the Fourth of July."

If there were no torrential rains, no summer drought, no damaging hail, no diseases in the corn, and after the first frost of the fall, it was corn picking time.

When I was very young I remember my dad picking corn by hand. He had a strange looking device. It was a hook that he wore in the palm of his hand, which was attached by a leather strap. It was called a husking hook. It looked like an oversized bottle opener. Dad used the hook to slice through the corn husk with his left hand, as he grabbed the

The farm wagon with the bang board attached, sitting next to the manure spreader.

ear of corn with his right hand, snapped it from the stalk, and tossed it into a wagon which was following alongside him. The wagon had one side built up high to keep the ears of corn from going over the wagon. Dad called it the *bang board*. The ears of corn *bang* into the board before falling into the wagon. It is also referred to as a bank board. The process sounds long, but Dad did it very quickly in one fluid motion. Think of it in slow motion: hook through the husk, grab the ear of corn, snap it from the stalk, toss the ear of corn over your shoulder, and the ear of corn hits the tall side of the wagon with a bang and slides into the wagon. Corn is literally flying through the air. My dad went down the rows of corn picking one ear of corn at a time. Later, corn harvesting was done by machine.

After the corn was picked it was hauled by wagon, later by truck, up near our house and put in corn cribs. The corn crib I am familiar with was a large circle of narrow boards about an inch apart held together by wires. As the corn was put into the enclosure, another circle of wire was added on top. The cribbing looked like snow fencing. This type of enclosure allowed the air to circulate and dry the corn before it was sold. The corn cribs changed the dynamics of the farmyard, like gaining new neighbors with massive houses. I felt closed in, as though the farmyard was getting smaller.

Corn cribs full of harvested corn on the Smith farm.

Another cash crop on the Smith farm was wheat. The wheat crop was usually harvested around the Fourth of July. I remember two machines being used to bring in the wheat crop, a binder and a thrashing machine. A binder is a machine that cuts the wheat and binds it into bundles, sometimes called shocks. The bundles of wheat were, at a later time, sent through a thrashing machine to separate the grain from the rest of the plant.

The two machines were later replaced with a combine, creating a big change in wheat farming. What I remember about the combine was the large rotating wheel, called a reel, on the front of the combine. It looked like a giant monster eating as it pushed the tall wheat plants into the cutting blades. A combine is a machine that combines the cutting and thrashing of the wheat. The grains of wheat are sent to a storage tank located at the top of the combine. The straw and chaff are released through the back of the combine and scattered in the field.

Using an attached auger, the wheat was loaded into a truck and hauled to a storage bin. A second person, usually one of my brothers, drove the truck because the combine needed to keep harvesting. Breakdowns did occur and had to be fixed quickly. Many times, my mom made a quick run for parts to repair the combine.

Larger wheat farmers hired wheat harvesting crews because the large modern combine harvesters are so expensive. The crews would start in Oklahoma, come up through Kansas, Nebraska, and into South and North Dakota, harvesting thousands of acres of wheat. My brother, Bob, had a farm in Wilsonville with large fields of wheat. I remember him talking about hiring a harvesting crew. Bob had to schedule a date early in the season and then hope the wheat would be ready to harvest on that date.

The things I particularly remember about wheat harvesting were the urgency to get it harvested, the long days, no stopping to come home for meals, and at dark the combine was left in the field right where it was stopped. Also, my father was very careful not to let the cattle eat the wheat because it could cause bloating. I also recall going with my mother to deliver meals to the wheat field. For me, it was like a picnic.

Neighbors helped each other prepare for winter. In the fall, our neighbors came to help fill the silo with silage to feed the livestock during the winter months. Corn stalks, cane stalks, and other foliage were chopped up to be used as silage. Putting the fodder in the silo allowed it to stay moist and ferment. Fermented silage was easier for the livestock to digest. The memory I have of this yearly event was the men washing up outside before coming into the house for dinner. I helped with this. I got a dishpan, set it on a bench in the front yard, placed the garden hose close by, brought out a bar of soap, and hung a towel on the fence. The crew cleaned up and was ready for a great dinner. Mom prepared fried chicken, mashed potatoes, gravy, green beans, and freshly baked pies. My part was to set the table and help serve the meal. On the farm we had breakfast, dinner at noon, and a lighter supper in the evenings.

Dad and his Case tractor.

A farm implement that my dad used was a Case tractor. The family just referred to it as "The Case." Dad used it to pull machinery through the fields. The Case tractor was used to run augers and elevators to get the crops into storage bins. Dad loved his old Case tractor. I am sure it was his first real tractor. The old Case went down the road so slowly; opened up to top speed, it went about 5 mph. I could walk faster. As the bright, new, green John Deere tractors began replacing old tractors, Dad preferred his Case tractor for many of the farm jobs. After the Case tractor's prime, Dad used it to pump water from a pond to irrigate farm crops.

In addition to the house, there were a number of other buildings on the farm, great when playing hide and seek. A windmill stood proudly in the yard with its giant wheel spinning and changing direction as the wind blew while pumping water for the livestock in the corrals. There was a weathered barn that was divided into sections to house pigs, newborn calves, and horses. Upstairs was the haymow filled with sweet-smelling hay. What fun we had playing in the hay. The barn was surrounded by numerous corrals and a tall round silo.

When electricity was available at the farm in 1945, a giant black pole was erected in the middle of the farm property. At the top of the pole was a very bright light. The yard light bathed the entire farmyard with a bright glowing light. Wires were strung to the pole and brought wonderful electricity to modernize life on the farm. A wire ran from the pole to the house to power lights and appliances. Another wire ran to the barn for the electric milking machines.

A white granary for storing newly harvested crops was part of the farm. A section was added to the building to store the old Case tractor.

The most interesting thing in the granary was a small machine called a corn sheller. I put an ear of popcorn in the top, turned the crank, and out came the shelled popcorn. The cob came out an opening in the back.

There was a hen house for the hens laying eggs. The hen house had nests filled with straw as a place to lay eggs and roosts where the hens slept at night. My brother, Duane, told me that the chicken coop was an old church. I remember the high fancy windows at each end of the chicken house.

Norris pulling the wagon with Margie in the farmyard.

The brooder (small chicken house) was for baby chicks. Looking back, I picture my dad bending over to enter the brooder house because it was so small. Each year Dad bought baby chicks that were shipped from a hatchery to the local feed store. The chicks came in specially designed cartons with holes in them. It was so much fun to hear and see the new baby chicks when they arrived. I could hear "peep, peep, peep," coming from the boxes. The chicks looked like little yellow tennis balls with legs.

There were also a couple of rickety garages and, when I was very young, an OUTHOUSE. We did get indoor plumbing when I was four or five.

The farm had a cave which had many uses. When a bad storm was bearing down on us, the family went to the cave to wait it out. The cave had a heavy, flat door with a large handle covering the opening. It had uneven cement steps leading down into the cave. It was cold, gloomy, musty, and very scary to me. Home-canned fruits and vegetables, potatoes and carrots from the garden, and some fresh fruit from the orchard were stored in the cave. It was a curse worse than death if Mom would ask me to go to the cave to retrieve a jar of peaches, pears, cherries, beans, applesauce,

*Beside the green Dodge and under the yard light: back row, **Joan**, **Joyce**; front row, **Carole**, **Margie**.*

beets, or pickles for a meal. I did it while looking for bats or snakes. My father installed a generator in the cave to produce electricity for parts of the farm.

Besides the regular farming, cattle feeding, raising chickens, and the dairy, we had a large garden. Everyone in the family weeded and picked vegetables. My least favorite garden job was picking up the potatoes after my dad dug them out of the ground. It took a lot of potatoes to feed our large family.

In our garden, there was a large patch of cucumbers. We had fresh cucumbers in the summer, and my mother canned dill pickles and sweet pickles. I remember bending over and looking through the thick vines to find cucumbers to pick. If the cucumbers were too large or turning yellow, Mom did not use them to make pickles. Instead of throwing them away, I carved boats out of the cucumbers. I used a knife to hollow out the center and create a boat. My brother, sister, and I had races with our cucumber boats in the horse tank.

Carole in her Easter outfit
beside Norris' Willys Custom Aero,
with the chicken coop in the background.

I have a vivid memory of my mother sitting and holding a large pan of water full of peas or beans freshly picked from the garden. Her hands moved so quickly and gently as she snipped each bean and podded all the peas.

One year the garden produced a huge crop of peas. Unfortunately, peas have to be podded, shelled. They were podded by opening the pod and removing the peas before they are canned or eaten. It was going to be an overwhelming and time-consuming job. Not sure who had the brilliant idea, but the wringer on the washer was used to shell the peas. My mother spread clean sheets around the washer to catch the peas. The wringer on the washing machine was adjusted, and pea pods full of peas were fed through it. The pea pods opened and peas spilled out. It was a funny sight, watching little green peas popping out of the pods and rolling down from the wringer. I remember pea pods in the washing machine. Mother canned the peas, and I am sure we ate — and ate — peas all winter.

Our family tells an anecdote about my sister-in-law, Norma's, gardening technique for planting her onions. Norma is my oldest brother Bob's wife. Norma loved onions and planted numerous rows of onions in her garden every year. Instead of bending over to make a small hole for each onion plant she put in the ground, Norma put on her high heels, went out to the garden patch and poked the holes with her spiked heels. The family thought this was the most ingenious idea for gardening.

My brother, Duane, had hives of bees in one of the many areas of

Bee smoker.

trees around the farm. I remember Duane getting ready to tend the bees. He wore a couple of layers of clothing, gloves, and a type of mesh helmet to protect him from bee stings. He also carried a smoker. A smoker is a covered, tin container with bellows attached. Duane would put rags in the tin and light them on fire. The rags smoldered and created smoke for calming the bees. The bellows added air that kept the fire burning and sent out a puff of smoke while Duane collected the honey from inside the hive. The honey was so delicious on home-baked bread.

A country prank was stealing watermelons. Finding a patch of watermelons in the middle of a field of corn was the goal. Swiping a few watermelons was expected, but some pranksters went too far and destroyed watermelons by splitting them open and leaving them to rot in the field. Dad planted his watermelon patch in the middle of a corn field off the main road to avoid carloads of teens finding his watermelons. My friend Ann remembers going out with friends and stealing watermelons. She insists that she sat in the car during the escapade.

Charlie *(Dad) in the corn field.*

I remember my dad picking a pickup load of watermelons and selling them to local grocery stores. I loved how Dad could tell if a watermelon was ripe. He would thump on the watermelon listening to the sound. Then he would thump on the bottom of his shoe. If they sounded alike, the watermelon was ripe.

When I was young, Dad had a crop of sugar cane. It was planted in a field quite close to the house, and I went into the field to get a stalk of sugar cane. It tasted like pure sugar. The best candy you could ask for.

There was an orchard near the house. It was fun to pick the apples.

Norris and **Margie**
with one of Dad's watermelons.

I would usually go down to the orchard to pick a few apples for my mom to bake a pie, apple crisp, or apple cobbler. My brother, Norris, and I usually picked them together. Norris climbed up the tree to get some of the high apples. I picked the ones I could reach from the ground. My dad and older brothers used a ladder and picked the remaining apples in the fall.

The farm buildings were surrounded by a large pasture, large corn fields, cane fields, wheat fields, a slough, and two lakes called Twin Lakes.

Looking back, I am amazed my mom and dad could organize all the numerous activities and jobs of running the house and farm. It took our large family to keep it all going, but Mom and Dad knew who, when, where, what, and how to get it all done. I don't recall a long to-do list, notations on the calendar, or sticky note reminders. They kept a running calendar in their heads and successfully ran our home and farm.

My Farm Chores

Chasing Chickens, Feeding Calves, Raking Hay, and More

My chores as a child were to help out on the farm. My sister and I washed all the bottles for the milk. We inherited this chore after our older sisters, Joyce and Joan, left for college. This whole process was done in the basement. My father made most of the equipment, and it was quite interesting. He mounted a brush horizontally to a motor attached to a wooden table. To wash the bottles, I dipped the bottles into a pan of hot sudsy water, inserted a bottle onto the moving brush, held the bottle while the rotating brush washed it, and then put the bottle into a pan of hot water to rinse. My father made a

The Smith cattle in the corral waiting to be fed.

drying rack for the bottles. It was a two-tiered stand on legs with large holes for the bottles. The holes in the boards were the right size to insert the bottles upside down and not fall through the holes. At the peak of production, we washed over 50 bottles every night.

After my father filled the milk bottles, he sealed them with cardboard bottle caps and set them in a tank to cool. My mother ordered the bottle caps by the tube from the Sears catalog.

Carole and I also had to wash the two electric milking machines every morning and night. We took the milking machines apart and washed the pieces individually. Washing the separator parts was a pain. Inside, the separator had at least thirty little disks that had to be washed. If I got a little sloppy, Dad made me rewash them.

Sometimes, I had to herd the cows up from the pasture at milking time. The pasture was down the hill from the corral and barn. The dairy cows were quite well trained and usually walked up to the corral without incident, but from time to time one of them was a little stubborn, and I had to run after her, yell, and wave my arms to get her going in the right direction. Sort of like herding kids.

Chores pertaining to chickens were not fun. One chore I had every evening was gathering all the eggs the hens had laid that day. I did not like gathering eggs because the hens would peck me while I reached under them to collect the eggs. I liked it when the hens voluntarily got off the nest and left the eggs neatly sitting in the straw. But there were always a few hens that stubbornly continued sitting on their eggs, prepared to peck at me to defend their eggs. I tried to prod them off by poking them with a stick with little success. The last course of action was just to grit my teeth and reach under the hens and gamble on not getting my arm pecked.

Also, at night the chickens needed to be closed in the hen house because of the coyotes looking for a tasty treat. I tried to avoid my dad when he was looking for someone to shut the chickens up for the night, but frequently I got the job. Most of the hens were already inside roosting. But just like kids, one or two decided to stay out after dark. I had to chase them around and around to get them in the hen house so I could shut the door.

The hens were not in pens, so they had free range of the whole farm. A few chickens wandered into the barn, hopped up the stairs to the haymow, and built a nest in the hay. I did not look for eggs in the barn every day, but my dad often reminded me to check for eggs in the barn. The hens chose not be obliging and lay the eggs in plain sight; they found secluded areas to lay their eggs. I confess that I did not thoroughly search the whole haymow looking for eggs. Consequently, I found a few nests full of green, stinking, rotten eggs. I tossed the rotten eggs out the haymow door to the pigs. Pigs eat anything.

When eggs were in abundance on the farm, my dad sold eggs to Clark Creamery. My sister, Carole, and I both remember washing the eggs. It was a nasty job. Down in the basement I got a pan of water and an old rag to wash chicken poop off the eggs. (No rubber gloves – YUK!) The cleaned eggs were stored in a rectangular crate with dividers, waiting for Dad to haul them off to the creamery.

Another yearly chicken chore I hated was moving the mature chicks from the brooder house to the chicken house so they could lay eggs. My dad caught the chickens by their legs and then handed them to me about four at a time. I carried those miserable chickens by the legs with their heads hanging down from the brooder house (back chicken house) to the chicken house. It was at least a city block by today's measurements. Of course, the chickens hated this and were constantly lifting their heads and pecking my hands. I dared not drop them because it was very difficult to catch them again. CHICKENS!

A chore I did from time to time was to feed milk to the cute baby calves. The calves were separated from their mothers and kept in a separate part of the barn with an adjoining corral. I went into the pen and fed the calves from a bucket of milk. As I went into the pen, the calves pushed and shoved, nearly knocking me down, trying to get their heads into the bucket of milk. Once in a while for my own safety, I stood outside the pen and fed the calves over the gate. It was hard to make sure each of the pushing and shoving baby calves got fed.

For fun, my older brothers tried to ride the older calves out in the corral. Each calf would buck up and down like a bull at a rodeo, with my brothers hanging on for dear life. I was too cowardly to try riding myself but laughed watching my brothers riding the bucking calves. It was like my private rodeo.

Another chore that I loved and hated was raking leaves in the yard. It was a large yard with lots of trees. It seemed like it took forever to rake all of leaves that had accumulated on the ground, but what fun it was to jump and play in the huge piles of leaves when we were finished.

Frequently, I helped rake alfalfa in the hay field by riding on the hay rake behind the tractor. After the alfalfa was mowed, the hay was left on the ground to dry. Then it was raked into piles or rows. My job was to sit on the seat of the hay rake and pull on a rope that brought the rake tines up so it would leave a pile of hay. Then very quickly, I lowered the rake tines so they began raking more hay. The hay was raked into piles, and my father gathered it to feed the cattle. I recall getting a really nasty sunburn while helping rake the hay.

My high school friend Ann recalls coming to the farm to help hoe the corn so she could work on her summer tan. We were oblivious to the dangers of UV rays, and sunscreen was not a word in our vocabulary.

My sister, Carole, and I both remember being recruited to help set siphon tubes in the cornfield. In the middle 1950s an irrigation canal was available for some of our cornfields, and I learned the art of setting siphon tubes. A siphon tube is a plastic tube used to irrigate rows of crops. The tube transfers water over the bank of the irrigation canal into the crop rows. To set a siphon tube, I placed one end of the tube into the water, covered the other end with my hand, and used a pumping motion to get the water moving in the tube. Quickly, I laid the siphon tube over the bank and into the row of corn. If I didn't get it the first time, I kept trying. The correct timing comes with practice.

As my sister and I struggled setting siphon tubes, my dad and brothers set tubes all down the cornfield rows. As the season progressed, Carole and I set siphon tubes much more quickly. My brother, Norris, boasted that he remembers setting 70 tubes per minute during irrigating season.

The summer before I went to college, my dad gave me one-third of the profit from a cornfield to pay for my college tuition. It was my job to help lay the sprinklers to water the cornfield. The job consisted of taking one end of an eight-foot pipe and carrying it over several rows of corn, then setting it down, and attaching it to another piece of pipe all down the length of the cornfield. The sprinklers would be attached, and that portion of the field would be watered. This same task was done a number of times to get the whole field watered. The field had been an alfalfa field for several years. Alfalfa puts nitrogen into the soil, and nitrogen is great for growing corn. As a result of frequent watering and the nitrogen in the soil, the corn grew very fast and very high. Did I also mention that I had to wear long pants and long-sleeved shirts to keep from getting cut by the corn leaves?

About the second or third time I watered the corn, it was well over six feet high. It was very hot and humid in the cornfield. While helping with the sprinkler pipes, I passed out from the heat. My father, being very protective, did not think I should continue helping. My brothers had to finish laying the sprinkler pipes for the season. Of course, I still got the money. My brothers gave me a hard time about it.

Every night I had to wash or dry the dishes. Those were two separate jobs, and one had to be very quick not to get stuck with always washing the dishes. We tried to take turns, but there was always a fight. Just as we got started, someone always had to go to the bathroom. The Smiths coined a phrase, "dishwater diarrhea." Of course, not wanting to cheat a sibling out of the pleasure of doing the dishes, we just waited to do the dishes.

When I was a teenager, my job was to dust all the furniture in the dining room before I could go to town on Saturday. I especially remember dusting the top of the buffet because the silver candy dish was sitting in the middle on a doily. I would procrastinate, then quickly dust. I tended to dust around the candy dish instead of moving the dish and doily when dusting. I was in a hurry to get to town. Now, that same candy dish is on a shelf in my house, accumulating dust. Fond memories.

Town of Cambridge

Recalling Soda Jerks, Milk Deliveries, and the Two-Headed Calf

Though I lived on a farm southeast of Cambridge, many of my memories are of Cambridge, a small town located between the Republican River and Medicine Creek and about 25 miles from Kansas. Cambridge had several names. It was Medicine Creek, then Pickleville, and in 1880 the Burlington Railroad reached the town and renamed it Cambridge. It was incorporated in 1885 and had a population of 200. When I was born in 1940, Cambridge's population was 1,084.

Cambridge had two disastrous floods – the Republican River in 1935 and the Medicine Creek in 1947. Lives were lost, and a significant number of homes and businesses were destroyed or damaged in both floods. The town survived and rebuilt both times.

The businesses in Cambridge served not only the people of Cambridge but also the large rural community surrounding the town. The only street that had a name in Cambridge was Main Street. There was no street sign; it was just called Main Street. And, yes, as a teenager I used to cruise up and down Main. Most of the stores were on Main. In my youth, Cambridge had two restaurants, two movie theatres, two drug stores, three grocery stores, a shoe store, a jewelry store, two banks, a city locker, a furniture store, a barber shop, a hardware store, a lumber yard, a local weekly newspaper, and a telephone company building.

There was also a tavern, but I never ventured in there. I peeked through the dark and smoky windows and saw men and a few women *drinking*. I perceived the tavern as a rather spooky and shady place. I was not acquainted with this aspect of life, as there was no liquor at the Smith house. (I am sure my brothers smuggled in some beer as they got older.)

Cambridge had three filling stations (gas stations.) My father patronized the Co-op Oil Company. It was a cooperative owned and managed by members. My dad was on the board of directors at one time. At the end of the year, profits were distributed to the members. There were pumps to fill cars with gas, and the Co-op also delivered gas to the local farms. On the farm, the gas was stored in large tanks and used for farm tractors and trucks. To buy gas for the family car at the Co-op, I pulled up to a gas pump, and a gas station attendant pumped the gas. He also cleaned the windshield and checked the oil. There were no self-service gas stations. When the attendant finished, I would cheerfully state, "Charge it to Charlie Smith," and be on my way.

The Cozy movie theatre burned down when I was quite young, so I remember going to the picture show (movies) at the Ritz Theatre on Main Street. The Ritz had a small lobby with a ticket booth and a giant popcorn machine. The popcorn machine was in front of a large window; I could see, smell, and almost taste the yellow, delicious popcorn as I walked by the theatre. Inside the lobby, swinging doors with tiny round windows led to a dark hallway and down a sloping aisle with seats on each side.

Also, on Main Street was a barber shop with a red-and-white barber pole out in front. I recall peeking in the window and spotting Dad sitting in one of the barber chairs with a cape around his neck, getting a haircut. Girls did not venture into the barber shop. It was a male place. The Barber Shop has been at the same location since 1884.

My favorite *hangout*, Bellamy's Drug Store, was on Main. The drug store dispensed prescriptions, had shelves of giftware, and a soda fountain. The soda fountain had high stools where I could order a malt or a shake and watch the soda jerk make it. The term "soda jerk" is in reference to the waiter pulling the soda draft arm. The jerking motion coined the name soda jerk. The soda jerk had containers of ice cream, syrups, and a malt machine. Usually I sat with my friends in the small

booths and had a Coke. Malts and shakes were expensive for my meager budget.

We used the term druggist instead of pharmacist. The druggist, Mr. Bellamy, prepared prescriptions in the back of the store. The raised prescription dispensary had a large window so Mr. Bellamy viewed his entire

Working side of a soda fountain used for making malts and shakes.
Courtesy of Cambridge Museum.

store. He appeared to be guarding his store.

John's Drug Store was also a fun place to go with friends. Instead of booths, John's had small round wooden tables and wooden chairs with round seats. John's specialty was cherry Cokes. I remember sitting on the wooden chairs drinking my *pop*, yakking non-stop with friends, and hoping a cute boy would come in the store.

As a teenager, I brought film from my Brownie Hawkeye camera to John's Drug Store. The drug store sent the film to a lab to be processed. I could hardly wait for photos to come so I could see them. I remember looking at the pictures the minute the clerk handed them to me. I was disappointed because some of the pictures were blurry or too dark.

Taking pictures was sort of a gamble; some good, some were bad, but I kept trying.

Cambridge had a soft serve ice cream store, similar to a Dairy Queen, called the Daisy Creme. The Daisy Creme had two walk-up windows to order ice cream treats. The windows had a sliding screen on the bottom, and the ice cream cone was handed out through the opening. During the summer, I remember swarms of bugs circling the lights above the windows. When I got my ice cream cone, I grabbed it very quickly, or the ice cream would have bugs on it. Looking back, it occurred to me that moving those lights would have saved a lot of ruined, buggy ice cream cones.

Another fascinating building on Main Street was the Telephone Company Building. As I peered in, a lady (operator) was sitting on a chair in front of this large panel and inserting wires into holes. She was wearing large black earphones and a black mouthpiece that looked like the mouthpiece on our telephone. She was in constant motion, plugging … unplugging.

When I called on the telephone at home, I used the small crank on the side of the phone to create one short ring, the operator in town would kindly ask, "Number please," I would say my friend's telephone number, and the operator connected us. My friends and I had some of the same conversations that modern teenage girls have on their cell phones: boys, classes, what to wear, who said what, who is going with whom. Some things do not change.

First National Bank.
Courtesy of Cambridge Museum.

My father did his banking at the First National Bank in Cambridge. The First National Bank building was built in 1910. C.M. Brown served as president of the bank from 1887 to 1951. Mr. Brown would loan money to farmers and businessmen based on their character. He assisted many farmers during rough times.

I remember my dad announcing, "Need to go see my banker." Sometimes I went with him into the bank. To a small child, the bank seemed very elegant. The floors were polished and shiny, and the walls had beautifully stained wood. I remember looking up at the tellers and perceiving them as being in tall gold cages and peeking their heads out to speak to my dad.

My favorite store in Cambridge was Thorndike's, owned by Harry and Ada Thorndike. They moved into the building in 1920. The Thorndike store was open for business in Cambridge for 70 years. It was a small-town department store. Thorndike's had very high ceilings covered with tin. Thorndike's sold groceries, apparel, shoes, giftware (china, crystal, and other items suitable as gifts,) and dry goods, (fabric and accessories).

Thorndike's.

I spent a great deal of time wandering around the store while my parents were busy getting groceries and chitchatting. Thorndike's had two entries, the alley and the street. My dad delivered milk and picked up the empty bottles at the alley entrance. I remember a freight elevator in the back of the Thorndike's. It was used it to haul merchandise to and from the basement. It went up and down using a rope and pulley. I never rode on it, but it looked very fascinating. When the elevator went down, it looked as though part of the floor disappeared.

The Smith family had an account at Thorndike's, and we charged everything. The clerk wrote the item and the price in a little book that had carbon paper. The purchases were wrapped in brown paper that came off a big roll of paper at the end of the counter. The clerk tied the bundle with string that came from a big roll. (No paper or plastic question.) While at Thorndike's, sometimes we kids talked Mom or Dad into buying us a nickel ice cream bar for a tasty treat.

The upper level of the Thorndike building has a long and unique history. It was originally the lodge for the Independent Order of Odd Fellows. Their symbol is incorporated into the architecture on the front of the Thorndike building. Later, the upstairs of Thorndike's was referred to as Thorndike Hall. Dances were regularly held in the hall. My sister-in-law, Norma, remembers going to

The Oddfellows symbol on Thorndike's.
Courtesy of Cambridge Museum.

Inside Thorndike's, this is the men's part of the store.
Courtesy of Cambridge Museum.

Rural Youth Organization dances in Thorndike Hall. An interesting footnote of Thorndike Hall pertains to the big band leader Glenn Miller.

According to an article by editor Alan Gaskill in the Cambridge Clarion of October 14, 1982, Glenn Miller spent time in Cambridge playing in a band. After World War I, Tommy Watkins, a native of Cambridge, hired a trombone player named Glenn Miller in addition to other musicians and started a band. The band practiced and performed in Cambridge. Before leaving on a tour of Texas and other western states, the band gave their final Cambridge performance at Thorndike Hall. The dance floor was packed, the entrance stairway was full, and others listened to the Tommy Watkins band while standing in the street. Cambridge boasts that Glenn Miller played in their town.

As I entered my teens, I sought the *latest* fads, in small town Nebraska. Marline Togs was a ladies' and children's ready-to-wear store. The name of the store, Marline Togs, combined the names of the owners, Marjorie and Pauline. The store opened in 1948 on the front porch of their parents' home and later moved to a room adjoining John's Drug Store. Marline Togs offered the latest fads in the teenage world.

Marline Togs clipping from the Cambridge Clarion. Courtesy of Cambridge Museum.

My friends and I loved going into Marline Togs. We admired all the stylish clothes, costume jewelry, and the latest stuff that was in style. I remember buying a bracelet that looked like a dog collar. My friends and I also purchased leather bullet boxes. They were ammunition boxes for soldiers.

The hardware store I remember in town was called Minnick's. Minnick's had counters and shelves full of tools, spools of wire, fat spools of twine, farm implement parts, and countless other items needed for the home and farm.

My father's cream can label.

What I remember about Minnick's Hardware was the enormous collection of tilted bins full of bolts of every size.

When I was quite small, I remember going to Clarks Creamery. My

Cream can.
Courtesy of Arapahoe Museum.

father sold cream, milk, and eggs to the creamery. Clarks Creamery was at the end of the block and had an ascending driveway. On the side of the driveway were double doors. Dad left his cream and milk at the double doors. At the creamery, the cream was put in 5-gallon cream cans (tall, galvanized steel cans with tight-fitting lids) and taken to the train depot. The filled cream cans were loaded on what we called the *milk train* and delivered to the Oxford Creamery. Milk train was the name given to a slow-moving train that stopped at every town along the railroad line. The creamery in Oxford produced butter and cheese.

Duane remembers that my dad began cutting out the middleman

and delivering his own filled cream cans directly to the train. My brother has one of the original cream cans labeled with my dad's name.

There was a feed store on the highway in Cambridge. The feed store sold bags of chicken feed. Customers bought chicken feed, washed the sacks, and used the fabric sacks to make clothing. I remember a cute sundress Mom made me using a chicken feed sack.

In the spring, Mom and Dad ordered and picked up boxes of noisy baby chicks at the feed store.

Lloyd's Clothing carried men's clothing and had a complete line of shoes for the family. I would admire all the shoes in the window, contemplating what shoes I wanted for school next year. After all the window shopping, I got saddle oxfords.

The Cambridge Museum holds fond memories for me. It was built in 1938 by the W.P.A. (Works Progress Administration was an employment program created by President Roosevelt in 1935.) I remember going on tours of the museum. One display stands out in my mind … the two-headed calf. I remember seeing it as I walked up the stairs. The calf seemed to stare at me out of one of its four eyes. In 1990, Cambridge built a new building and moved the museum. When I returned in 2017 to visit the new museum, my first question to the curator was, "Do you still have the two-headed calf?" I was excited that it was still there.

Cambridge Depot.

Two-headed calf in the Cambridge Museum.

I remember attending Brownie Scout and Girl Scout meetings in the basement of the old museum. I joined Brownie Scouts in third grade. I recall feeling proud to wear my Brownie uniform to school on meeting days. Another memorable day was graduating from Brownies to Girl Scouts. I felt so special lighting my little candle during the ceremony. Although our troop did not participate in selling Girl Scout Cookies, I remember the delicious cookies our mothers provided for snacks at the meetings.

Eva (Perdue) Smith (in front) and her club members
in line to tour the Cambridge Museum.

Saturdays and Sundays
on the Farm

Going to Town, Church Services,
and Sunday Dinners

Saturday night was a major social event of the week. The stores in Cambridge stayed open until 9 p.m. When I was young our family *went to town* on Saturday night. Dad parked the car on Main Street. He had to get there early to get a good parking spot. In town on Saturday night, my mother shopped for a few items, then sat in the car and talked with her lady friends. My dad went to the hardware store or the car dealership to shoot the breeze with the guys. But, WOW, the kids got to walk the streets of Cambridge, actually, just up and down Main Street. *Everyone* came to town on Saturday night. The kids chattered, giggled, and ran up and down the sidewalks. As I got older and had a little spending money, I sometimes went to the picture show (movies.) At 9 p.m., the town, as we said, "rolled up the sidewalks." (The stores closed and everyone went home.)

The first picture show I remember going to at the Ritz theatre was "Snow White." I walked out in the middle of the movie because it was too sad. I left several movies because they were sad, but apparently I grew up. When I was a senior in high school, a group of friends and I went to the drive-in movie in McCook and saw "The Hand." I drove out to the farm by myself after the movie. I was terrified that *the hand* was coming over the seat to attack me. I kept glancing over my shoulder to make sure there was not a hand ready to get me. It was a terrifying drive.

My favorite picture show as a teenager was "Carousel." It is a musical about a young, innocent girl who falls in love with an unsavory, but good-looking guy, working for the carnival. It starred Shirley Jones and Gordon McRae. I loved the music and was intrigued with the main character Billy Bigelow. He was shady, but he loved Carrie. The song "You'll Never Walk Alone" was incredible. Hearing the song gave me goosebumps.

Debbie Reynolds and Pat Boone were my favorite movie stars. In the '50s, celebrities were not in the news all the time. We did not hear movie star gossip on talk shows or the news. Debbie Reynolds starred in the kind of movies I liked, musicals and romantic stories. It was rumored that because of his marriage, Pat Boone would not kiss a girl in a movie. My friends and I watched him in romantic movies … waiting and hoping to see him kiss the girl. He got close, bent his head down, and NO kiss. As I look back, it was probably just a public-relations ploy to attract young girls to his movies.

On many Saturday nights my mom and I listened to the Hit Parade on the radio. The Hit Parade was sponsored by Lucky Strike cigarettes and was referred to as the Lucky Strike Hit Parade. The radio show played the top tunes of the week, saving the most popular three songs for the end of the show. Mom and I made a list of the most popular songs of the week for my sisters, Joyce and Joan. My sisters were out on Saturday nights with their friends and couldn't be bothered with listening to the show themselves.

Saturday night was hamburger night on the Smith Farm. On Saturday, Mom baked bread and made large hamburger buns for Saturday night supper. To make her great burgers, Mom cooked large hamburger patties on the griddle. Now I tell you, it does not get any better than home-grown, corn-fed beef on a freshly baked bun topped with a homemade pickle. McDonald's should have consulted my mother about great hamburgers.

While my mother was baking bread, I would churn butter in the large glass churn. There was a crank on top of the churn that twirled the wooden paddles. Mom poured thick cream into the jar to make the butter. As I turned, and turned, and turned the crank, the butter formed. Mom drained the buttermilk, salted the butter a bit, and we had home-churned butter for the freshly baked bread.

When I was a kindergarten teacher, I made butter with my students. I poured whipping cream into small baby food jars, put the lids on tightly, and had the students shake, shake, shake, until butter formed. Terrific science project … changing matter from one state to another.

On Sundays as a family, we attended the Methodist Church in Cambridge. In addition to church on Sunday, the Methodist Church was a big part of our family's community life. The church was the place for celebrations, numerous dinners, banquets, marriages, and funerals. There was Sunday School for the kids. As a teenager, I was active in MYF, Methodist Youth Fellowship. After the Sunday church service, the adults would stand out in front of the church and talk, talk, and talk about the week's happenings. I was sitting in the car anxious to go home and thought they would never quit gabbing.

Families sat together for the Sunday church service. The Methodists had quite large families, and some families occupied most of the pew. At the time, we joked that the Methodists had larger families than the Catholics.

A fond memory of sitting in the church pew with my family was looking over during the sermon and seeing my Dad … SLEEPING? I never did hear him snore, thank heavens. He gave the excuse that he was just resting his eyes … Sure!

On Sunday nights I attended MYF. Not sure how much religion was discussed, but it was a fun group. My brother, Norris, my cousins, Dick and Larry Moore, and my friend, Ann Easter, were part of the MYF. We had functions with MYF groups in other towns. Later at college, I remember meeting a couple of boys from the Arapahoe MYF.

Historically, Methodists were teetotalers. The United Methodist Church has taken a more liberal stance on abstinence, but the church still supports temperance. Communion at church was grape juice. At 13 years of age, I clearly remember sitting in the third pew on the left side of the Cambridge Methodist Church and signing a pledge that I

The Methodist Church, built in 1923.
Courtesy of Cambridge Museum.

would abstain from alcohol. I have a twinge of guilt as I drink an occasional glass of wine.

The founders of Welch's grape company were good Methodists as well as savvy businessmen. They saw a huge market in supplying grape juice for communion in temperance-minded churches.

1944 — Cambridge Methodist Church Sunday School.
Margie Smith *kneeling front row, left;* **Norris Smith**, *sitting second from right.*

Rev. Lewis Schultz, a minister at the Methodist Church in Cambridge during the late 1950s, was from Boston. Rev. Schultz and his family made the trip from Boston, Massachusetts, to Cambridge in an old rickety car. Rev. Schultz remarked the family thought they took the wrong road in Nebraska. For miles they saw only cornfields, pastures, fences, no visible signs of life, and no towns. They were thankful to finally arrive in our small town of Cambridge.

The Schultz's moved into the parsonage, a two-story, white house with a large front porch, next to the church, and slowly adjusted to small town life. The church members became accustomed to his Boston accent and welcomed him with food and donations for his house. The picture I have in my head is Rev. Schultz standing behind the pulpit wearing a long black flowing robe. Previous ministers did not wear a robe. Rev. Schultz was a supportive advisor for our MYF group.

I secretly wondered why anyone would leave a big city like Boston for a Podunk town in Nebraska. It shows how little I understood about the appeal of living in a small farm community.

Sunday was always an entertaining day when I was growing up. We usually had company for Sunday dinners: aunts, uncles, and cousins. When relatives from out of town were visiting, there was always a large Sunday gathering. Always eating and talking! In Spanish, "sobremesa" means conversation after the meal has ended with the people you shared your lunch or dinner. As a kid, I remember Sunday after-dinner conversations that lasted well into the afternoon. As the kids in the Smith family have families of their own, we sit around the dining room table after a meal having great conversations. It is a wonderful family tradition.

Ice cream freezer.

My favorite Sunday activity was getting a block of ice at the ice house after church and making homemade ice cream. Dad loved ice cream and enjoyed making it. Mom mixed the ingredients while Dad was getting the ice ready. Dad put the block of ice in a gunny sack, (a burlap bag used to transport grains, potatoes and other agricultural products) and used the side of the axe, and pounded the ice into small chunks. Dad was absorbed in crushing the ice. He pounded the bag of ice as if conducting an orchestra: adagio – long slow movements, allegro – lively and fast, with intervals of staccato – short sharp taps. I was fascinated as I watched.

My mother poured the ice cream mixture and put the wooden paddles into the ice cream can. Outside, Dad put the ice cream can into the old wooden ice cream freezer and attached the cranking mechanism.

He packed ice around the can and topped it with salt. Then, Dad steadily began turning the handle. The Smith kids volunteered (volunteering is doing a job without complaining) to turn the crank on the old freezer. When the handle was hard to turn, that meant the ice cream was freezing. Flavorings were added: strawberries, peaches, and the Smith family favorite ... Grape Nuts. After the ice cream was mixed and frozen is the best part ... taking out the paddles. Why is this a best part? Because I got to lick the ice cream off the paddles! Licking the paddles was sneaking a little taste of the delicious ice cream, like licking the spoon and bowl after making cookies. The freshly made ice cream was packed in ice, waiting to be dessert.

Many Sunday afternoons, I escaped to the basement, turned on the radio, and listened to my favorite radio show, "The Shadow." Its famous beginning, "Who knows what evil lurks in the hearts of men? The Shadow knows." The musical theme followed, then an extended spine-chilling laugh. I was captivated and ready for another mystery. The Shadow had the power to cloud men's mind and become invisible. I pictured the scary scenes in my mind as I listened on the radio. The scariest part of the show was the announcer's voice. He absolutely gave me goose bumps, but I kept listening. I still am partial to good mysteries, reading them or watching them on television.

We usually had relatives at our house for Sunday dinner. I remember earning some spending money on Sunday afternoons by washing relatives' cars. I would use the garden hose and a bucket of soapy water. I charged a dollar per car. My dad even helped by recruiting customers for me.

Gambles store in Cambridge sold a large variety of products: small appliances, dinnerware, paint, household gadgets, and lots of toys at Christmas filled the shelves. In this photo, I see many products similar to kitchen items I remember: a waffle iron, an angel food cake pan, a meat grinder, and large kitchen scales.
The man on the right is my classmate Karol's father, Ed Taylor, one of the owners of Gambles, along with Tom Aiken, on the left.
Courtesy of the Cambridge Museum

Feeding the Smith Family

Home Grown and Home-Made Delicacies

Most of the food for our family was raised or grown on the farm: cattle, pigs, sheep, chickens, apples, cherries, pears, potatoes, sweet potatoes, carrots, green beans, peas, cucumbers, lettuce, radishes, beets, onions, tomatoes, watermelon, musk melon (cantaloupe), and popcorn. The cattle and chickens provided us with milk and eggs.

When I was a child, my favorite meal was my mom's great fried chicken, corn on the cob, and mashed potatoes and gravy. The recipe for terrific fried chicken is a cast iron skillet, lots of lard, and fresh chickens. It is hard to duplicate that recipe today. Meals at the Smith house were home cooked and served family style. I don't remember going out for meals when I was a kid. There were no fast food restaurants and very few restaurants in Cambridge. Dad was quite frugal, and taking the family to a restaurant to eat was not in his DNA.

Chicken gizzards were a favorite part of the chicken at my house. The gizzards never made it onto the chicken platter. Someone always got a fork and ate the gizzard right out of the frying pan. When my older brothers were no longer at home, I did the deed.

The Smith family preferred dark chicken meat. As the platter of chicken was passed around the table, the legs, wings and thighs were the first to go. Being one of the younger Smith kids, I got one of the last pieces of chicken on the platter, the chicken neck. I learned to enjoy the meat on that chicken neck. My older brothers took all the thighs, wings, and legs just to tease me. My mother tended to sacrifice the good pieces and ate the chicken back.

Breakfast was usually at different times because my dad got up early to start the morning chores. I remember my sister and I having breakfast together. Besides the oatmeal and Cream of Wheat that my mother cooked for my sister and me, shredded wheat was also a staple for breakfast. Each box of shredded wheat contained 12 loosely woven pillow-shaped biscuits. I loved reading the cardboard dividers that separated the layers of shredded wheat. The cards had so much information printed on them. That was the start of my habit of reading the newspaper, now my iPad, while eating breakfast.

Our family usually had supper, the evening meal, together at the table. The exception was Sunday evening. You were on your own for supper. I remember Norris making himself an egg sandwich. It looked like scrambled eggs on bread with plenty of catsup. It looked and smelled so good!

My mother spent much of the summer and fall preparing food for the winter. The cherry pitter she used to prepare cherries to be canned stands out in my memory. Mom clamped the cherry pitter to a wooden table in the basement, poured in some cherries, turned the handle, and out would come pitted cherries. I am sure it was not that simple, but that is how I remember the process.

My mother canned fruits and vegetables: peaches, pears, cherries, applesauce, beets, green beans, corn, sweet pickles, and dill pickles. She bought fruit by the bushel basket from the local grocery store. Mom always waited for the Colorado peaches. She preferred the Colorado peaches over the California peaches. Other produce came from the garden and orchard. Potatoes, carrots, and apples were stored in the cave. I remember eating fresh apples during the winter.

To get the fruits and vegetables ready for canning, Mom cleaned, peeled, snipped, podded, cut, and sliced or diced all the fruits and vegetables. She put the prepared fruits and vegetables in Mason jars and screwed on the lids. Mom loaded the jars into an enormous pressure cooker. After the pressure cooker was heated and built up pressure, Mom placed a weighted gauge on top of the pressure cooker. And, the SHOW started. The gauge was noisy as it jiggled, rocked, hissed, released steam, and went up and down. In my young mind I was sure it was going to blow up, but no big bang. Mom carefully removed the jars from the pressure cooker. I heard a POP as the jars sealed.

Mom made dill pickles, and that was another process. Large stoneware pickle crocks full of cucumbers, dill, and brine sat on the counter for days until they were pickles. She used large gallon jars for the dill pickles. I remember relishing those big, yummy, crunchy dill pickles.

Jars of canned fruits and vegetables were on shelves in the basement and in the cave. I never counted, but I'm sure over 100 jars of food were canned and ready for winter meals on the Smith Farm.

To provide meat for our meals, my father took a steer, or sometimes a pig, to the Cambridge Locker Plant. The Locker was a huge walk-in freezer with floor-to-ceiling rows of lockers, (enclosed bins and drawers). Customers rented lockers for their frozen food. The bottom lockers were pull-out drawers.

The rear of the Locker Plant had a butcher shop, a small office, and a place to pick up keys for the lockers. The Locker Plant had an alley entrance for delivering the livestock. The butcher, my Uncle Stub, would slaughter the animal, prepare the meat, cut and wrap the meat in packages, mark each package, and then place the packages of meat in the correct locker. Our family rented a large drawer in the Locker Plant.

While in town, we stopped by the locker to get meat for our meals. When it was my job to get a package of meat from the locker, I recall shuddering at the thought of going into the huge and cold locker room. I remember the locker being a scary place. The heavy, thick, clanging locker door would close behind me as I went into the locker. I felt a shiver of fright as the locker door closed, leaving me alone in the locker. My hands were freezing as I frantically rummaged around the large freezer drawer looking for the meat Mom requested. I was always happy to open the heavy locker door and leave that spooky place. When I talked to my brother, Norris, about this, he remarked that he had the same eerie feeling about the locker room. He believes going into the locker to fetch meat for supper is why he is a little claustrophobic.

My mom rendered lard after a pig was butchered. The fat from the pig was boiled until brown cracklings rose to the top of the pan, then the mixture was strained. According to the dictionary, cracklings are the crisp residue left after the rendering of the lard. My memory of making lard is Mom using a strange-looking black lard press to separate the lard from the cracklings. The lard press was stored in the basement. Carole remembers the smell of rendering lard. It lingered in the air for hours. After the lard rendering, Mom put the lard in jars and used it for cooking. I do not remember when she quit rendering lard and started using Crisco, but I recall a big can of Crisco sitting on the counter when Mom was baking.

I remember coming home from school and seeing large circles of thin noodles hanging over wax-paper-covered kitchen chair backs to dry. Mom was making noodles. Making noodles also brings to mind Mom's dented, well-worn flour sifter with a little crank on the side she used when baking. After she sifted the flour and added the other ingredients, she mixed the dough for noodles with her hands; it looks like playing with Play Dough. With plenty of flour on her hands and the counter, Mom began rolling out the dough using her well-used old wooden rolling pin. She rolled the rolling pin back and forth over the dough until it was as flat and thin as paper. Then Mom dried the noodles on chair backs before cutting them into long strips of noodles. She used the homemade noodles to make soup or my favorite, chicken and noodles.

After Mom and Dad purchased a freezer, my mother and Aunt Dorothy prepared sweet corn for the freezer. Preparing the corn was a daylong process. My dad picked enough sweet corn to fill the back of his pickup truck and parked the load of sweet corn under a shade tree in our farmyard. My cousins, Dick and Larry Moore, along with Norris, Carole and I, shucked and cleaned every ear of corn. We were the genuine *Nebraska Cornhuskers*. We spent all morning husking, teasing, and chattering. Several ears of corn had a black fungus, smut, on them. It looked so yukky, none of us wanted to shuck that ear of corn. But, groaning and holding our noses, we did. We cut the smut off with a knife and continued shucking. My mother and aunt would boil the corn, cool it in tubs of ice water, cut the corn off the ear, put it in plastic bags, and put the prepared corn in the freezer. The corn was delicious on those cold Nebraska winter days.

During all of the mayhem of getting the corn prepared, *miraculously* a lunch of fried chicken, corn, and mashed potatoes was prepared for all of us. How did my mother do all of that?

Mom also froze fresh peaches after we bought the freezer. I love frozen peaches. Mom got a bag of frozen peaches out of the freezer and set them on the counter for the family dessert. Just when the peach slices started to thaw and were still a little icy, I would begin sampling them. It was like eating peach ice cream. One little partially frozen slice at a time, I would devour nearly half the package. Mom scolded me, about eating most the peaches. The family could eat the thawed peaches left in the package; I liked them when they were icy.

On the Smith farm, we had a lot of fried chicken. My sister, Carole, and I helped with preparing the chickens. Our role in the process was plucking the feathers. The dead chickens were dunked in scalding water. The feathers absorbed the water and made it easier to pluck the feathers. My mom called it picking the chickens. Most of the feathers came out in clumps, but the tail and wing feathers were tougher to pluck. Carole and I pulled and pulled to get them out. Mom would dress the chickens. Dressing the chickens refers to cleaning, removing innards, and cutting the chicken into pieces. Mom filled a large section of the freezer with the cleaned and dressed chickens. I watched but never wanted to learn the process. My mother's fried chicken was delicious! The chicken tasted even better in the middle of winter.

Popcorn was a favorite snack on the Smith farm. Dad planted a small area of popcorn in the cornfield. I liked to help shell the popcorn using the sheller in the granary. I popped popcorn in an old blackened popcorn popper on the stove burner. There was a handle on top of the popper to stir the popcorn as it was popping. The vents on the top of the popper spewed out hot grease and burned my arm as I stirred madly while the kernels popped. The burned arm was soon forgotten as I delved into the tasty popcorn. Occasionally, my mother would make fudge to go with the popcorn. Good stuff!

Another snack that was really special was flavored pie crust. When my mother made her delicious pies, there were leftover pieces of pie crust. She sprinkled cinnamon and sugar on the leftover crusts and baked them for us. It was a tasty treat.

I remember the first time I ate pizza. Pizza was not a familiar word or food to me. For a rural Nebraska kid in the 1950's, there were no Pizza Huts or pizza joints. For my 16th birthday party, my mother cooked something new, pizza pie, for my friends and me. It was unusual but tasted great. My friends and I loved it. Thus, started my love of pizza. Two years later, at college, I was introduced to Valentino's Pizza in Lincoln.

I belonged to a 4H Club. The first recipe in the 4H cookbook was cinnamon toast. I mastered cinnamon toast. I worked my way up to making apple crisp. I don't remember entering any of my food in the county fair.

Even though my mother was a fantastic cook, I did not cook very often. I do recall one bizarre cooking experience. My parents went to the State Fair in Lincoln, and I was home with my older brother, Bud. I decided to cook fried chicken for him. I knew that you had to flour and brown the chicken, but I was unaware that it needed to cook longer. So, I browned it and gave Bud the beautifully browned chicken to eat.

Eating watermelon on the Smith farm.
Left to right: **Bob***, MaryAnn Teeter, Don Perdue,* **Joan***,* **Norris, Joyce, Duane***, Bonnie Perdue, Glenn Brooks,* **Margie***, Dick Moore, and Larry Moore.*

When he took a bite, it was still raw on the inside. Yuk! Not every farm girl learns to cook.

Most of my relatives lived in or around Cambridge. When out-of-town relatives came for a visit in the summer, we had a picnic at the City Park. Picnics meant fried chicken and potato salad carried to the park in the picnic basket, which I now possess. No paper plates or plastic silverware. Each family had to tote their own dishes and silverware, then hopefully the kids got the dirty dishes into the correct picnic basket after eating the picnic lunch. When the celebration was at the Smith House, there was watermelon! The kids ate it outside and had watermelon-seed-spitting contests.

Stalwart Ancestors

Overcoming adversities
to build homes in a new land

A ll the things that have gone before remind me of my ancestors and their struggles to become successful. They set the character for our generation as hardworking farm families. My forebears labored to make my life easier, and I enjoy the best days of my life because of the past strengths of my kinfolks.

I admire the tenacity of my ancestors. Emiline Lea Perdue moved to Cambridge with her five children to prove up on a homestead after the death of her husband. At 20 years of age, Alfred Ovenden journeyed from Kent, England, to Elk Creek, Nebraska, and

My great-grandfather Joseph Clark Perdue, (b. 1845 d. 1882).

established a substantial farm. Sherman Smith left his family farmstead in Kenesaw to establish his own family farm near Cambridge after his father was killed by an exploding steam engine. Mary Gardiner, whose father was a Holland whaler, left Ireland to come to America. My family history builds bridges between the generations of my relatives.

"To forget one's ancestors is to be a brook without a source, a tree without a root." This Chinese proverb explains why I cherish the history of my ancestors.

My maternal great-grandparents were featured in an article published in the "Cambridge Centennial Book." "Joseph Clark Perdue was born in Abbington, Illinois, and married Emiline Lea who was born in Mississippi, and moved to Lincoln, on a farm located at what now is

Joe Perdue is on the far left in the back row. Pictured are: top row from left, Joe Perdue, Julia (Nolan) Corder, Lula Sipe, Will Nolan, Maria Nolan; bottom row from left, M. A. Ellingson, Fred Nugent, Tom Nolan, Mrs. Ellingson, Mrs. James Nolan, Etta (Nolan) Proud, and Elizabeth Nolan.
Courtesy of Cambridge Museum.

14th Street. In the early 1880's Mr. Perdue took up a homestead about 3 miles east and 4 miles north of Cambridge. He returned to Lincoln to get his wife and children and took sick and died while there. His wife, Emiline Lea Perdue, and her five children came out to the homestead and lived in a dugout for a short time and later made and moved into a sod house, later adding a frame second story. The family consisted of John, the eldest who was 16 when they moved to the homestead, Lura was 14, Jessie was 12, Frances was 8, and Harry Clifford (Joe,) the youngest child, was 6."

In 1885 Emiline Lea Perdue proved up on the Certificate of Ownership which was signed by President Chester Arthur.

My grandfather, Harry Clifford (Joe) Perdue, son of Joseph Clark and Emiline Lea Perdue, was born in 1878 in Lincoln. He died in 1947 in Cambridge when I was only 7 years old. I remember that Grandpa Perdue played the guitar. He also wore a hearing aid. It was quite large and Grandpa carried the battery unit in the front pocket of his overalls.

1935 – Joe and Emily Perdue's farm, east of Cambridge.

Joe Perdue, top left, and a group of Cambridge men.
Courtesy of Cambridge Museum.

Joe Perdue, top left, and the same group of Cambridge men 50 years later.
Courtesy of Cambridge Museum.

*Wedding picture of
Harry (Joe) Perdue and Emily Ovenden,
1902.*

*My great-grandfather, Alfred Ovenden,
(b. 1825 d. 1913).*

My grandmother, Emily Viola Ovenden (Perdue), daughter of Alfred and Sarah Jane Erwin Ovenden, was born in Elk Creek in 1886. She died in 1982. She was the ninth child and the only girl. She was only nine years old when her mother died of tuberculosis. She lived in Elk Creek with her father and eight older brothers.

Quoting from my Grandmother Perdue's journal, "My father was a good, honest man and a Christian. He had two farms and owned 360 acres of land. He was considered a well-to-do man at that time. The place was owned by an Ovenden for over 100 years."

Harry Clifford (Joe) Perdue and Emily Viola Ovenden were married in 1902 at Cambridge. Quoting from Grandmother's journal, "When I was 15, I went to Cambridge and stayed with (older brother) Crandol and wife and went to school one term. There I met Joe Perdue. We wrote letters when I went back to Elk Creek. Many times, I had to iron several shirts or such for my brothers before they would give me my letters from Joe. The next Christmas, Joe spent in our home at Elk Creek, and we became engaged. The following September when I was just 17, we were married at Crandol's. We were so in love. I think Joe was the kindest man in the world, and we were so happy. I never regretted my marriage. Joe was very good to me. We were never very rich but happy. Joe was very musical and sang and played the guitar, but his hearing was never good and became worse as time went on. We had so many happy times. Our family was healthy, we had picnics, a trip to the mountains with Dolphs (her brother's family) when the children were all home. We had hard times too. We paid our groceries with milk and also raised lots of truck garden (that is, vegetables), and the children could all help with that, even selling watermelons to tourists on the highway. We always had a watermelon patch, and the kids in town all knew it. Many of them tried swiping them at one time or another. If Joe caught them, he would bring them to the house and make them eat melons till it came out their ears."

Quoting from my Grandmother's journal of her religious beliefs at the time, "At that time, I didn't believe in playing cards. The boys brought home a pack, and I hid them. Now I realize it isn't the cards, it is what they are used for that is bad, but I never learned to play. Also, dancing was a sin to us, and we had some unpleasant rounds with the kids over this." In 1948 Grandma wrote in her journal, "Just a year ago today he (Joe) left us so lonely and sad. There have been many heartaches and lonely hours the past year, but have so much to be thankful for. He didn't have to live and suffer for months when there was no hope of getting well. I am fortunate in having children who are interested enough in me to be kind and good to me. I am so glad my health is good so that I can keep my home. For all these things I am truly thankful and hope and pray that I can find contentment in the future."

Children of Joe and Emily Perdue. Clockwise from top: Eva, (Mom) Clark, Dorothy, Dale.

I have many memories of my Grandma Perdue. I spent nights in town with her and enjoyed helping make breakfast. I was fascinated with Grandma's toaster. I opened the sides of the toaster using the cute little handles and put a slice of bread in each side. When one side of the bread was toasted, I opened each side, turned the bread around, and toasted the other side. I guess you had to be a 7-year-old girl to think this was so much fun. Maybe it was because we didn't have a toaster at home, or it was the store-bought bread at Grandma's. My mother baked our bread at home.

Grandma Perdue loved to crochet. She crocheted doilies, pot holders, doll dresses, pillows, and lace edging for pillowcases. Every grandchild got a fancy set of pillowcases with her crocheted lace as a wedding gift. Grandma Perdue crocheted beautiful dresses for my Shadow Box Dolls. She taught me to crochet in the evenings when I stayed at her house. I remember making a long chain of pink, crocheted yarn.

Part of Grandma's house was converted into apartments that she rented. There was one bathroom in between, which she shared with her renters. I enjoyed visiting with her renters when I was at Grandma's house. One renter, an older lady, invited me into her apartment for cookies.

Grandma Perdue was always interested in her grandchildren and attended all of our school and church functions. She was an avid gardener and planted her garden every year until her death in 1982. Every Saturday Grandma Perdue made a Jell-O salad and brought it to Sunday dinners, which could explain my aversion to Jell-O.

My paternal grandfather, Sherman Ellsworth Smith, son of James Albert and Susan (Frame) Smith, was born in 1873, at Elkhart, Indiana.

My great-grandparents farm,
James Albert (b. 1840 d. 1884) and Susan (Frame) Smith (b. 1843 d. 193?)

The Shurigars:
back row: Millie, Mary, Agnes; front
row: John Sr. (b.1829 d.1917), John Jr.,
Margaret Catherine (my Grandma
Smith), and Mary (Gardiner) Shurigar
(b.1837 d.1905.)

He died in 1950 in Cambridge. My grandmother, Margaret Catherine (Shurigar) Smith, daughter of John and Mary Shurigar, was born in Luzerne, Iowa, in 1877. She died in 1957. Grandma Smith's mother, Mary Gardiner, was born in Ireland.

My grandparents, Sherman Ellsworth Smith and Margaret Catherine Shurigar, were married in 1894 at Kenesaw. They later

moved to a farm south and east of Cambridge. The farm was not far from where our house would be. Grandma Smith had what we now call osteoporosis, which gave her a hump on her back. I remember going to their house on Sunday evenings, and Grandma Smith would make popcorn for all of us. Grandpa Smith was a little gruff and wore a black wool coat. His black coat hung on a hook by the back door.

After Grandpa Smith died, Grandma Smith moved in with a daughter, Bernice. Because of

1894 - Wedding picture, Sherman Smith
and Margaret Shurigar.

disagreements over financial settlements, we no longer associated with Grandma Smith. What a shame! I feel I missed so much by not being allowed to spend time with Grandma Smith. Of course, no one talked about the problem. My father did reconcile and forgive his mother and sister before Grandma Smith's death.

I had lots of aunts and uncles. My father was the third of seven children. Three of my father's sisters and their families moved to Boulder, Colorado. My mother was the oldest of four children. One of my mother's brothers lived in Rock River, Wyoming. The rest of the families lived around Cambridge. I was delighted to have a large extended family: aunts, uncles, and cousins, all living in or near Cambridge.

My aunt, Dorothy Moore, Mom's younger sister, seemed more *with it* than Mom. She was quite artistic, loved to sing, and did a lot of

1945 – left to right: Sherman and Margaret Smith, **Charles Smith,** **Robert (Bob) Smith,** **Eva Smith,** *Emily and Harry (Joe) Perdue.*

crafts. She taught me how to textile paint. I painted flowers on a dish towel by using a stiff brush, fabric paint, and a stencil. I gave a dish towel to my mother as a gift. Mom liked the pretty towel, and I remember using it to dry dishes.

Aunt Dorothy went to the drugstore and had her daily fountain Coke. (When I was young, drug stores had a soda fountain; you could sit right at the *bar* on seats that twirled, or there were also a couple of booths or tables.)

When I was old enough and asking questions about sex, my mom gave me some pamphlets to read and then told me to go talk to Aunt Dorothy. I learned about female *things* from Aunt Dorothy.

I admired my uncle, Glen Moore. He was Aunt Dorothy's husband. Uncle Glen was very nice and seemed really interested in what I was doing. He was a carpenter and cabinet maker. He built many of the

*1944 – Children and grandchildren of Joe and Emily Perdue. Back row, from left, Crandol Ovenden (Grandma's brother), **Bud Smith**, Isabelle Perdue, **Bob Smith**, **Charles Smith**, **Eva Smith**, Ethyl Perdue, Glen Moore, Dolph Ovenden (Grandma's brother); middle row, **Duane Smith**, **Joan Smith**, **Joyce Smith**, Bonnie Perdue, Dorothy Moore; front row, Dale Perdue, **Margie Smith**, Emily Perdue, Joe Perdue, **Norris Smith**, Donnie Perdue, Dick Moore, Larry Moore, and Clark Perdue.*

houses in Cambridge. He was also active in the Methodist Church Choir.

If I had a school activity in the evening, I would go to Aunt Dorothy and Uncle Glen's house after school, have dinner (we called it supper), and stay until it was time for the school activity. On my visits to Aunt Dorothy's house, we often had pancakes with peanut butter. I loved staying in *town.*

Smith is a family surname originating in England. It is the most prevalent surname in the United Kingdom, Australia, and the United States, particularly among those of English, Scottish, and Irish descent. The name refers to a smith, the Old English term meaning one who works in metal.

1944 – Perdue Cousins:
*Back row, from left, **Joan Smith**, Bonnie Perdue, **Bob Smith**, **Bud Smith**, **Duane Smith**; middle row, Donnie Perdue, **Joyce Smith**, Dick Moore, Larry Moore; front row, **Norris Smith**, and **Margie Smith**.*

The family surname Perdue is recorded in several spelling forms including Pirdue, Pardoe, Perdy, and Perdue. This surname is medieval English but of Norman-French origins. The development is a form of a favorite oath in pre-10th century Old French, "Par Dieu," meaning "by God" but anglicized to a *sound like* spelling.

Other surnames in our family are Shurigar and Frame on the Smith side and Ovenden and Lea on the Perdue side. All of the Leas immigrated to Virginia and some families changed their name to Lee. Maybe Grandma Perdue was right that we are related to Robert E Lee, the Confederate general during the Civil War.

*Grandma and Grandpa Perdue
in June 1943.*

*Great-grandmother Susan (Frame) Smith,
(b. 1843, married 1866, d. 193?).*

*Perdue cousins in 1938: back row, **Bob Smith, Duane Smith, Bud Smith;**
middle row, **Joyce Smith**, Bonnie Perdue, **Joan Smith;**
front row, Dick Moore, Larry Moore, and Donnie Perdue.*

My *Childhood*

Quarantine, Music Lessons, Family Cars, and Kid Games

W hen I was a child, most homes were two-parent homes, mom and dad. Most mothers did not work outside the home. Available jobs for women were traditional women's jobs: secretary, teacher, nurse, librarian, etc. Families ate supper together and life was more relaxed. A family had one phone and one television. Kids respected their elders, there were few drug problems, and a really bad word was *damn*, BUT there was racism, sexism against women, and a fear of communism.

I had the normal childhood diseases, measles, mumps and chicken pox. Immunizations were not available when I was a child. The kids in our family tended to have illnesses in groups. I remember having scarlet fever at the same time as my brothers and sisters.

For two weeks in May (I forget which year,) this quarantine sign hung on our house to warn people that we had scarlet fever.

Scarlet fever patients were quarantined, which meant that we had this red sign nailed to our house; only my father could leave the house. Numerous things we used while we were ill had to be burned.

The picture is of the quarantine sign that was on our house. My sister, Joyce, saved the sign in her scrapbook. We were quarantined from May 2 to May 16.

Most of my brothers and sisters had their tonsils taken out at the same time. I missed that group *tonsillectomy party*. I was too young; I still have my tonsils intact. I did join my brothers and sisters eating ice cream, even though my throat was not hurting from having a tonsillectomy.

When I suffered with an upset stomach, I got to drink pop … 7 UP. It was the only time I remember having pop when I was young. As I recovered, my mother would make milk toast for me. She cracked an egg on a slice of bread, covered it with milk, and cooked it in the oven. Sounds terrible, but it tasted so good. What made it so great was my mom fixed it just for me.

I remember taking piano lessons when I was in grade school. Mrs. Baughman was my piano teacher. To remember the names of the lines and spaces, I used mnemonics. The treble clef lines were Every Good Boy Does Fine, and the spaces were F A C E. The base clef lines were Good Boys Do Fine Arithmetic, and the spaces were All Cows Eat Grass. It is unbelievable that I still remember them. Once a week, I trudged up the front steps of Mrs. Baughman's house and regretted not practicing the preceding week. As I sat down on the piano bench, I saw the foreboding metronome, taunting me to play at a faster tempo than I was prepared to play. The lesson began with practicing scales and a few pieces (songs) in review, then the selection that Mrs. Baughman had assigned for me to practice the preceding week. I gave a meager attempt at making the song sound melodious. Mrs. Baughman did not give out many encouraging remarks. Eventually, I convinced my mom to let me quit piano lessons. Later, as many adults do, I wished that I had continued my piano lessons.

I do not remember getting into trouble very often (selective memory.) My friend Ann and I tried to play a joke on my cousin Larry. During a church MYF meeting, Ann and I drove Larry's car a couple of blocks from the church. When the meeting ended, Larry came out to go home, and his car was gone. I'm sure Ann and I both looked guilty, and we quickly confessed to the prank. We were lucky Larry did not call the police. The Cambridge Police Force was one cop, and he was usually sitting in his car parked at the intersection of Main and the highway.

My dad had the final decision if we wanted to do something out of the ordinary. I would always ask Mom first, and if she thought it was OK, she would occasionally run interference for me with Dad. I can still hear her saying in her patient voice, "Charlie, I think we should let

Marjorie Lou Smith.

Margie ...." If Mom and Dad were both against what I wanted to do, just forget it. No way of talking both parents into that request.

From time to time, living in the country was lonely. One Saturday, I really wanted to go to a friend's house in town. Living in the country, I couldn't hop on my bike or walk over to my friend's house for the afternoon. Our family had only one car, and trips to town had a purpose, not to provide a taxi service. I decided to walk to town, secretly hoping a neighbor would come by and offer me a ride. Four miles is a long way! I remember making it all the way to the Republican River bridge before I got a ride.

The first car I remember our family having was a four-door 1938 Ford V8. My dad flipped a little silver switch before he pushed the small round starter button. No car keys needed. The gear shift was a long metal stick with a black knob on the top. I remember those things as if I were sitting in that car today. The trunk of the car had a strange little hump on it and was opened with a silver latch. I think of the many times my dad opened the trunk and put carriers of milk in it. I am told the car was maroon in color. I remember the paint on the car being so thin and faded that it looked blotchy purple to me. Mom did some reupholstering in the car. She used a royal blue material to cover the inside panels of the doors. I can still see that leather-looking cloth being so colorful in the old faded car.

That old Ford was our family car for 11 years. Cars were not manufactured during World War II. The car companies manufactured military equipment: jeeps, tanks, hardware, and airplanes. Everyone had to drive their old cars and deal with gas rationing.

The next family car was a green 1949 Dodge. Carole remembers the day Dad brought the new green Dodge home. Dad was so proud to have a new car. After riding around in the old faded purple car, he thought the new shiny car looked very stylish. The Dodge had a sun visor over the top of the windshield. The green Dodge is the car I remember driving. My older siblings had graduated, so my senior year I got to drive to and from school.

Bob and Bud were out of high school and had their own cars. Bud had a grey coupe that he parked in a garage in back of the clotheslines. It was a rickety looking old garage. It had probably been painted white at one time, but there was not much paint left on the boards. To get his car into the garage, he had to drive through the farmyard, take a sharp left, then go into the garage. The garage was so small that the car barely fit. The doors to the garage looked like two wooden gates. They swung together and were held closed using a two-by-four across both doors.

Norris remembers a 1951 Green Chevy pickup. The pickup was his mode of transportation before he bought his own car. Carole learned to drive the pickup. She drove around the farm before she got her driver's license. Carole passed on a story about the Chevy pickup. While backing it out of the garage, she cut the corner too short and took off a piece of the garage on her way out.

Do I remember any big fibs that I told? I take the Fifth. I am sure I told a few fibs but do not remember the consequences. Though I was not a perfect child, I was not a problem child. Our family did not have a lot of rules. If I did something wrong, you could be assured that my parents would find out and supply the consequences. Actually, a gruff word from my dad was punishment enough for me.

In my teens, I did not have a curfew. My dad would just say, "Be home early." My interpretation was probably before midnight.

Most of the fights between my brothers and sisters were about chores, washing the dishes, bathroom time, and who got the chicken legs.

AND, my brother, Norris, was infuriated because he had to wait on me every morning before going to school. I feel it was preparation for his future. He shows more tolerance as he waits on his wife.

I have fond memories of my mother's J.U.G. club. The club was started in 1928. A group of young mothers looking for female companionship met at my mom's house and made plans to form a club. The mothers brought their children to the meetings. The women chose the name "Just Us Girls," and it became known as the J.U.G. Club. The dues were 25 cents per year, and J.U.G. Club met every two weeks on Thursday afternoon. The women took turns hosting the meetings. Mom said the women helped the hostess with some of her hand sewing and had a great afternoon out.

The children outnumbered the women at their meetings. While our mothers were working and chatting, the kids were having a better time playing outside. My mother later told me some of the husbands were upset because the kids made a mess outside on the farm, but J.U.G. continued. As teenagers, we teased our mother about her "jug" club.

As their children grew up and had families, the club became "Just Us Grandmas." The members included their husbands for a potluck dinner and played pinochle.

Before television at our house, the primary source of news was the radio and the Omaha World Herald. The paper from Omaha was delivered to our house daily via the mail. We were five hours west of Omaha, but the mailman brought the Omaha World Herald the same day the paper was printed.

Kids of J.U.G. ladies.
Back row: Shirley Hilton, Dick Moore, unidentified, Sharon Johnson, unidentified, Larry Moore, Barbara Johnson, unidentified, Sondra Johnson, and **Norris Smith.** *Front row: unidentified, unidentified, Vivian Johnson,* **Margie Smith**, *and Larry Jones,*

I remember three things about the Omaha World Herald. Many of the news articles were accompanied by a little map pinpointing where the news had happened. I did not read many of the news items, but I did read the headline and was fond of looking at the map to see where the event took place. Today when reading or listening to the news, I miss the map showing exactly where the action took place. The second thing I liked about the paper was the picture pages. Every edition had a page or two of news pictures. I would look at the pictures and read the captions. As a child, it was my way of seeing the world. And of course, the World Herald had the funnies. I loved reading the funnies. When Dad was reading the paper in the evenings, he gave the kids the funnies. I remember reading "Blondie," "Mary Worth," "Little Orphan Annie,"

"Henry," "Steve Canyon," "Nancy," "Joe Palooka," "Gasoline Alley," and "Li'l Abner." Many years later, my teenage son, Scott, had a paper route and delivered the Omaha World Herald.

I was recently watching the BBC news. In honor of Remembrance Day, the British reporters were wearing poppies on their lapels. Suddenly a picture of my dad popped into my mind. Dad was returning home from town wearing a red crepe paper poppy.

Margie on her birthday with the granary in the background.

The stem of the poppy wound around the buttonhole of his bib overalls.

Wearing poppies was inspired by a 1915 poem by John McCrae, "In Flanders Field." The poem refers to how the poppies blow in the field where soldiers are buried. Poppies are an international symbol of remembering fallen soldiers.

My birthday was usually celebrated by family parties, friends invited for a slumber party, and always a home-baked cake or cupcakes. School started after my birthday, and that was always exciting. Starting back to school meant new clothes, new shoes, and reconnecting with my friends from town.

I did not get an allowance, but I did get money from my parents when I needed it, not necessarily when I wanted it. I had enough money to go to the movies occasionally or to have a Coke after school. I declared, "I got everything that I wanted; I was just smart enough to know what was possible to want."

My sister, Carole, has memories of asking Dad for spending money. He would give her money when she asked, but he had to tease her a little first. When she asked for some money, Dad would grin and remark, "Go work the other side of the street. I'm working this side." As he was talking, he would pull out his wallet and hand her some money, but my sister remembers being embarrassed when she was with her friends.

The one time I recollect being mad at my mom and dad was when they did not let me go to town on Halloween Night. No amount of begging helped. I sulked because I knew my friends were having so much fun running around town. Perhaps, my parents were aware of the pranks kids played on Halloween.

I remember milk and cookies with Mrs. Brown. Mr. and Mrs. Joe Brown were our closest neighbors on the farm. I walked over to the Browns for summer afternoon visits. My time with her was like a tea party. Mrs. Brown and I sat down at the kitchen table, she offered me tasty cookies from her cookie jar, and we chitchatted. Mrs. Brown seemed genuinely pleased as she answered my quiet knock at her door. My mom would not let me go as often as I wanted because she thought I was only going for the cookies. That was undoubtedly part of the reason, but I liked Mrs. Brown. Because her sons were grown, she enjoyed chatting with a little girl.

While researching Cambridge families in the Cambridge Centennial Book, I read about Mrs. Brown having a daughter that died at 3 months of age. I think Mrs. Brown liked me visiting because she missed having a little girl.

Mrs. Brown also gave me a little, black cocker spaniel puppy, and I named him Blackie. He was an outdoor dog, and I remember chasing Blackie as he ran all around the farmyard. Blackie wriggled as I petted his soft black fur; he wanted to run. Blackie was not very old when he was accidently killed. After my brothers finished using the pitchfork, they threw it over the fence and stuck the tines of the fork into the ground. One day, Blackie accidently ran under the pitch fork and got caught by one of the sharp pitch fork tines. I saw it happen. I remember him lying there so silent. It was very traumatic for both my brother and me.

When I was growing up, there were no computers, no computer games, no Nintendo, no Play Station, and no Internet. Kids of our generation used our imagination and played games with our siblings and school friends.

*My brother, **Norris,** and friends on his fifth birthday. **Norris** is on the far left, and **Margie** is in front and the only girl.*

One of my favorite outdoor games was Cops and Robbers. On the farm, we found rocks that looked like gold nuggets. To play Cops and Robbers, one kid would steal the gold from the bank, and the posse would chase the bank robber. Sort of like hide and seek, except the robber kept changing hiding places. After pursuing the robber, the posse captured the thief and took him/her to jail.

My younger sister, Carole, and I played outside in the summer. We pretended to cook by making all shapes and sizes of mud pies. The mud had to be just the right consistency to design all the shapes. We decorated the mud pies with leaves and old twigs and set the mud pies on an old discarded sewing machine stand in the back yard. Carole and I pretended we owned a bakery.

Another fun venture was making hollyhock dolls. The farm had a lot of pink blooming hollyhocks in the front yard. My sister, Carole,

Hollyhocks.

and I would spend a quiet summer afternoon designing our dolls. To make the dolls, we used a hollyhock bloom, removed the stem, and turned it upside down for a skirt. A blossom was used for the head and attached to the skirt with a toothpick or small twig. If Carole and I wanted to be fancy, we attached another bloom for a hat. The dolls were so beautiful in the eyes of young girls.

Hopscotch was another of my favorite games. We had no perfectly drawn hopscotch games outlined on the blacktop; we scratched our hopscotch game in the dirt. My friends and I took turns hopping up and down in the squares on two feet then one foot. We discovered a little key chain was much more accurate to toss than a piece of glass, a stone, or a coin. How many hours did I spend playing hopscotch?

I played Jacks with a small, red rubber ball and ten jacks made of metal. I tossed the ball in the air, picked up jacks, held the jacks, and caught the ball, all with one hand. One jack, then two, then three, until I picked up all ten jacks at one swoop. I practiced and was quite accomplished. I kept my jacks in a little drawstring bag and took them when I went to friends' houses. I learned not to leave any of those jacks on the floor because they were lethal if you stepped on one.

Another activity I adored was playing with paper dolls. A package of paper dolls came with a doll of thin cardboard and a separate sheet of paper with several colorful outfits for the doll. I cut out the clothes, very carefully making sure of cutting on the lines, then attached the beautiful clothes to the paper doll by folding tabs at the top of the outfit. Hours of fun! Virtual paper dolls on the computer are now popular. Just drag and drop the clothes onto a doll. Where is the fun in that? No cutting or anticipating how the gorgeous outfit will look on your paper doll.

I played marbles occasionally. It was more of a boy's game, but I did have some of my own marbles. Boys kept their favorite marbles in a bag and played games of marbles at recess. Everyone had their favorite shooter, an aggie or a steelie. To play marbles, we drew a circle in the dirt, put marbles in the center, and took turns shooting marbles out of the circle. In my day, kids played for keeps. You had to be a good shot, or you lost all of your marbles, literally.

Everyone had roller skates. I skated on the sidewalks, not at a skating rink. I liked to roller skate in town because there was only one short and narrow sidewalk at our house. Couldn't get much speed before the sidewalk ended. My roller skates clamped onto my shoes, and I carried a skate key on a shoe string around my neck as I was skating because I needed the key to tighten the skates around the soles of my shoes. There was also a bolt in the middle of my skates so I could adjust the length of the skates. I used those skates for years, then passed them on to my younger sister.

One year Carole got a little red record player for Christmas. It was like a little suitcase with a turntable, and it played one record at a time. Carole's record player was a favorite toy for a long time. I remember getting a record that was on the side of a box of cereal. After cutting out the record, we played it on Carole's record player. My sister and I played that record so many times, I am sure my parents were sick of it.

When I was very young, I received a doll for Christmas that cried "mama" when I picked her up. She was dressed in a beautiful pink dress, a matching bonnet, shoes, and socks. The doll was beautiful. The head was a hard plastic material. My doll's eyes opened and closed. Her crying mechanism was in her cloth body. After playing with her several months, my dolly was dirty, and I decided she needed a bath. Of course, when I got her wet, the crying part was ruined. Live and learn!

Our family played a lot of card games and board games, especially in the winter. I remember playing Monopoly with my brother, Norris, on long cold weekends. I enjoyed playing checkers. I also remember an old wooden board for playing Chinese Checkers, but we always were short a few marbles … the actual round playing type, not what you are thinking! We also had card games: Old Maid, Rook, Canasta, Slap Jack, and Rummy. My favorite card game was Old Maid. It was so much fun to put on a poker face when someone was drawing the old maid card out of my hand. The person holding the old maid card at the end of the game was the loser.

Brownie Hawkeye camera.

My favorite toy was my Brownie Hawkeye Camera. Taking pictures of my friends was exciting. They liked to ham it up for pictures. I used the flash attachment for indoor pictures. The flash was so bright, my friends saw spots after the flashbulb went off. I took my camera to slumber parties, birthday parties, and some football games. The camera was not cheap to use because I had to pay for film, flashbulbs, and processing. There were no instant pictures, there were no do-overs, and I had to wait at least two weeks to get my pictures processed to see the results. In the Midwest, the word picture usually sounded like pitcher. You would hear people say, "I took a pitcher."

I had a collection of what was referred to as Shadow Box Dolls. They were a popular toy. They were like Barbie Dolls but did not have movable arms and legs. The dollies were made for display rather than to play with. Grandma Perdue crocheted some beautiful dresses for the dolls. My dad made me a three-dimensional frame (shadow box.) I dressed the dolls in the green and pink dresses my grandmother had crocheted, arranged the dolls on glass shelves in the shadow box, and hung it on the wall of my bedroom. I liked sitting and gazing at the dolls.

Another favorite activity of mine was reading. I could spend hours curled up with a good book. My favorite book as a child was "Heidi." The main character, Heidi, lived in the mountains of Switzerland, a completely different county and environment than mine. I loved reading about Heidi's life in the Alps. Heidi became quite famous in the sports world. A game between the Oakland Raiders and the New York Jets on November 17, 1968, was remembered as the Heidi Game. At 7 p.m. NBC preempted the end of the game and aired the previously scheduled showing of the movie "Heidi." The Oakland Raiders came from behind and scored two touchdowns in nine seconds, but nobody saw the game-changing scores because the television audience was whisked away to the Swiss Alps and a little girl named Heidi.

I read teenage mystery stories, including the Nancy Drew and Ginny Gordon series. My favorite was "Ginny Gordon and the Mystery at the Old Barn." I read "Little Women," "The Secret Garden," "My Friend Flicka," and "Thunderhead." I regret that I did not read more of the classics.

A favorite game, or joke, was snipe hunting. Norris and I tried to convince Carole Ann, that we saw a snipe on the other side of the corn crib. She hunted for that snipe for a *long* time, while we played along with the joke and laughed at her under our breath. I remember my older brothers playing the same trick on me. My younger sister did not get to retaliate. She was the youngest.

As I was growing up, I heard how Bob had wanted to try out for the Major Bowes Amateur Hour, an American radio talent show. Bob was very talented at yodeling. Yodeling is a form of singing involving changing from high-pitched to low-pitched notes very quickly. I heard my brother yodel and liked the sound of it. My father discouraged Bob in his attempt to try out. My brother had been in the Navy and had traveled to many places in the world. My father had only been in Nebraska and felt secure on the farm. Making a living by playing the guitar and singing seemed very risky to my father. I wish my father had allowed Bob to try. I will always wonder.

When I was in high school, I designed a desk. I drew the plans for the desk to scale and planned the lumber and supplies I needed to make the desk. My dad went to the lumber yard with me, and we bought all the supplies. I ordered the wrought iron legs from the Sears catalog. My dad helped me build it, then I sanded and stained the desk. I remember sitting at my desk studying. My brother, Norris, liked it so much that he built a desk for himself. I used my desk all through high school. I now wonder what happened to that desk.

Most of my childhood memories revolved around family: Mom, Dad, brothers, sisters, aunts, uncles, cousins, Grandma Perdue, friends, and being raised on a farm near a small town. Looking back as an adult, I realize I had a great childhood. I had two parents that loved and trusted me. There were not many rules, but I did not want to disappoint my parents. Believe me, living in a small town, they would know! By today's standards, my life was sheltered and quite naïve.

Nebraska Weather

The 1947 Flood, Storms, Ice Skating, and Rowing in Circles

Nebraska has a wide range of weather conditions. The running joke about Nebraska weather is, "If you don't like the weather, wait 10 minutes, and it will change." There are rainstorms with brilliant lightning and deafening thunder, sweltering summer heat, high winds and tornadoes, raging blizzards with the wind making snowdrifts in the yard and fields, and beautiful sunny days.

Margie dressed for winter fun.

In the winter, I was always disappointed that the county road crew cleared the snow from our road so quickly, and we made it to town for school. All of the beautiful snow was piled in drifts just begging me to go outside and play, then I heard the snowplow coming down the road and spoiling all the fun. My dad was always relieved that our road was cleared and he was able to deliver milk to the grocery stores in town.

I vividly remember one clamorous summer thunderstorm. Carole and I were home alone on the farm as a rainstorm began to grow stronger and more ferocious. Each flash of lightning seemed closer and closer, and each clap of thunder was louder and louder. The rain was beating on the roof and windows. We were SO terrified that we hid under the bed out of sheer fright. Being the brave older sister did not count: I was the first to dive under the bed. As the intensity of the storm began to dwindle, I remember peeking my head out from under the bed to check things out. Slowly Carole and I slid out from beneath the bed and peered out the window. We sat tightly huddled on the bed until we heard a car. My older brother Bud came to check on us and the farm. We were so thrilled hearing his car pull into the farmyard.

Nebraska weather changes with the seasons. The cold and snow of winter gradually changes to the beauty of spring. Flowers begin blooming, farmers are planting corn crops, and baby calves are born. As

1947 Flood: Cambridge Main Street; note the Ritz Theater on the left.
Courtesy of Cambridge Museum.

122

the hot weather arrives, water activities abound: swimming, boating, and playing in the lawn sprinkler. In the middle of the summer, wheat is harvested. Fall arrives with cooler weather, school begins, and the beautiful yellow and red foliage appears. On the farm corn is picked.

The weather can also cause mayhem. Twelve years after the devastating flood of 1935, early in the morning of Sunday, June 22, 1947, a flash flood inundated the town of Cambridge. A wall of water came with no warning, catching Cambridge residents off guard. It had been a very wet spring, and the rivers and creeks were full. North of town, it rained eight inches in a 24-hour period and caused the Medicine Creek to overflow its banks and engulf Cambridge. The water was waist high on Main Street and up to 12 feet in other parts of town. No one could get in or out of town because the one highway going through town was submerged. A headline in the Cambridge Clarion of June 26, 1947, was, "Flood Takes 13 Lives." The paper noted that news stories were incomplete due to lack of space and time. The Clarion office had four feet of water over all the equipment, but the editor quoted the saying, "Despite h— and high water the paper must be out."

The country road, our route to town, was flooded. The pastures and most of the farmland were underwater. The cattle in the pasture had to swim to reach the farmyard pens. Many of the baby calves did not make it and were drowned. The farmhouse had been moved to higher ground after the 1935 flood and was not flooded. I remember standing on the road by our house, looking down the hill, and seeing the road to town filled with water. I saw and heard the water swirling around the bridge just a short distance from our house. The water was an ugly, dirty brown color.

Duane, 16 at the time, made a sorrowful discovery following the 1947 Flood. A day or two after the water receded, he rode on horseback to the pasture to repair fence posts the floodwater had damaged. While riding home, he saw the body of a small child in a mud drift about one-fourth mile from our house. Duane hurriedly returned to the house and told my mother about the drowned baby. Mom called the disaster headquarters, and they sent an ambulance to recover the body. My recollection of the incident was all the whispering and solemn looks of the adults. They were gathered in the stairway door, talking quietly so the younger children could not hear. I was 6 years old, but I sensed something very serious was transpiring. It was later that I heard about the drowned baby that my brother had discovered in our pasture.

The Medicine Creek Dam, which had been authorized years earlier, was funded and built in 1948-49, following the disastrous 1947 Medicine Creek Flood. The dam provides protection from potential floods. I remember all the construction workers moving to Cambridge to work on the Medicine Creek Dam. The townspeople referred to the workmen as "Okies." I recall Dad driving the family out to the dam site on Sunday afternoons to see progress on the dam. I was astounded at the size of the enormous cement structure across the creek bed.

One hot summer, there was an *invasion* of millers. (Miller moth is the term given to any moth that is particularly abundant around homes. Moths have fine scales that cover their body. The scales rub off as if the miller is dusty or dirty. They have the unusual habit of banding together in armylike groups.) Millers were swarming everywhere: around doors and windows, under the bushes, and in the grass as I walked. I have a vivid recollection of my mother bringing

Poster celebrating the Medicine Creek Dam. Courtesy of the Cambridge Museum.

in the laundry from the outdoor clotheslines. When she brought the dry clothes into the house, pants and shirts were filled with millers. My dad's overalls were filled with gray yukky millers. We took everything outside and shook the millers out of the dry laundry. Huge swarms of millers took off flying as we shook them from the clean clothes.

Power outages were a common occurrence on the farm, especially during storms, and we had to return to the days without electricity. My parents had kerosene lamps sitting on top of the kitchen cupboard for the frequent outages. Kerosene lamps have a wick as the light source, and the flame is protected by a glass chimney. When the electricity went off, my mother would light the kerosene lamps. Their light made a gentle yellow glow in the room. I would sit close to a lamp and read.

There were not a lot of things in the farmhouse powered by electricity, so a power outage was not a major catastrophe. The refrigerator was electric, but I do not remember having a lot of spoiled food. Much of the food was canned and stored in the basement. Milk was kept cold in a tub of cold water downstairs. Our meat was stored at the "locker" in town. The heat source for the house was a coal furnace, the cook stove used propane gas, there was always plenty of food, and our entertainment was reading or playing games. The radio was electric, so I missed my favorite radio show. If the outage occurred at milking time, it was a problem. Dad cranked up the portable generator or reverted to milking the cows by hand.

With time, the farm became more dependent on electricity. Many appliances were electric – television, large refrigerator, freezer, hot water heater – so power outages were more significant.

Two of my favorite activities during the winter were ice skating and sledding. We had a wooden sled with runners. My brother, Norris, and I went sledding on a small hill across the road in the Brown's pasture. We wore two pair of jeans, winter coats, hats, and mittens to stay warm and dry. But we usually came home from sledding cold and soggy. In town, there was a steep hill behind my Uncle Glen's house. We called it cemetery hill because it was adjacent to the cemetery. I used an inner tube to slide down that hill. Sliding down that long, steep hill was so much fun, but *oh*, … the long climb up the hill in preparation for another exciting ride down was not as much fun.

I have a batch of ice skating memories. Do not want to brag, but my friends thought I was a great ice skater because I could perform turns and spin in a circle while ice skating. My friends believed I was headed

for the Ice Capades. I had a pair of figure skates: shoe skates, not the type you clamp onto your shoes. My skates were hand-me-downs, but I thought they were great. I skated on the Twin Lakes (this was one of two lakes down in our pasture.) I had numerous skating parties during the winter. We used an old tractor tire filled with wood to make a fire. My friends and I would practice figure skating, play

Ice skating on Twin Lakes.

some ice hockey, and warm up around the fire. After spending the afternoon skating, my friends and I walked up the hill to my house for hot chocolate. Is there a reason why all of my memories end with food?

Another ice skating memory is Christmas Day when I was in the seventh grade. I went ice skating at the skating pond in Cambridge. As I was stepping over chunks of frozen mud to reach the ice, I fell and broke my arm. A lady at the park packed my arm in snow and drove me to my Aunt Dorothy's house. My parents were there for Christmas dinner. Doctor Stearns was out celebrating Christmas, so it took a long time to get my arm set and in a cast. Dr. Stearns took his patients to the hospital in McCook. Dad drove me to McCook, which is 25 miles west of Cambridge. Dad said he helped the doctor reset my arm. My dad was surprised how much strength was required to manipulate and reset the bone. Of course, I was out during this procedure. When I woke up, my arm was in a hard, white cast.

A broken arm *did* get me out of washing dishes and milk bottles for six weeks but *did not* get me out of school work. I broke my left arm, and, being right-handed, I could still write.

In Nebraska there is a lot of snow. When I was a kid, playing in the snow was so much fun. There were snowball fights, sledding, snow angels, finding clean snow to eat, building snow forts, playing fox and geese, rolling down huge snow drifts, wading in deep snow, and writing in the snow with a stick. My mother was not as thrilled with snow. When the kids came indoors, we were tracking in snow and making muddy puddles. There were wet clothes and boots cluttering and dripping on the floor.

Margie Lou on the snow horse.

The Smith kids made snowmen in the yard every winter. We used small pieces of coal for eyes, nose, and mouth. We used sticks for the snowman's arms. All the hats were in use, so the snowmen were bare-headed.

One year, my older brothers and sisters assembled an elaborate snow horse, and I had my picture taken sitting on it. They used an old coat for a saddle and used real reins. Other than getting a cold behind, I loved playing on the snow horse.

As soon as school was out for the summer, off came the shoes, and it was barefoot time. I had to be very careful around the farm not to step in chicken poop or get purple feet from walking under mulberry trees. The mulberries ripened, fell off the trees, and lay on the ground. The chickens were *free range* and wandered all over the farm. Naturally, they did their business everywhere, and did it ever stink. Yuk! I washed my feet with the garden hose and dried my feet by rubbing them in the grass before going into the house.

I remember Norris and I making a kite one windy spring day. There were no kits to buy for making kites. We made our own kite by taking one long thin piece of lightweight wood and a shorter one and attaching them in the middle by wrapping string around them. We secured a string around the outside to make the kite shape. Then we pasted newspaper over the outside string. For a kite tail, we ripped rags and tied them together. We did buy the kite string. Our kites were much heavier and were hard to get up in the air. I recall running at high speed trying to get the wind to catch the kite and then letting the string out quickly, so the kite would soar up into the sky. A lot of work, but so worth the time and effort. I am still fascinated with kites.

Another summer activity was horse riding. The Smith family had a horse named Beauty. I have asked family members about the story of the horse. No one seems to know. She was just part of the farm and named Beauty. The horse helped with rounding up cattle. My brother, Duane, remembers riding Beauty when he was herding sheep. My brothers and sisters and I all have memories of riding Beauty.

I rode Beauty to my friend Jackie Sayer's house. I didn't like to saddle the horse, so I made my little sister, Carole, do it for me. She was my little sister: isn't that

Beauty.

what little sisters do? Beauty was very independent; she walked in the ditches along the road even though I struggled to keep her on the road. Beauty also knew when she was close to home, because she took off galloping as we got near the house. I held on for dear life, and she got me home, then Beauty ran straight into the barn.

Also, Carole remembers riding Beauty and having to duck her head as the horse ran pell-mell straight into the barn when returning home.

One summer, I got my very own bicycle. It was a hand-me-down from a cousin, but the bicycle was repainted, so it looked new. It was a beautiful blue and white bicycle, and I adored that bicycle. Our country roads were not paved, so riding my bike took a lot of leg muscles to keep it going on the rough country dirt roads.

Margie with a bicycle.

I stayed cool in the summer by running through the sprinkler, standing in front of a small oscillating fan, or just sitting in the shade of a big tree while reading a good book.

One of my summer camping experiences was Girl Scout Camp. For the camping trip, troop members made beds using blankets – no sleeping bags – and slept on the hard ground. After putting on our pajamas and climbing into our bundle of blankets, we talked until the wee hours of the morning. *Fun!* I remember it as a grand time, except for going into the woods to pee. *Scary!*

Another camping experience was a week at Camp Comeca, a Methodist Church Camp in the hills south of Cozad. The campers slept in little cottages full of bunk beds. Meals were served in the dining hall, and everyone took their turn helping cook and serve the meals. The week was loaded with activities: swimming in the lake, playing softball, craft classes, hiking, discussion groups, and time to wander around the camp and talk with friends. I remember painting a nativity set. I was proud of the nativity set and kept it for years. I also recall climbing to the top of a hill called Inspiration Point. I could see for miles ... very inspirational! I also vividly remember being very homesick while at camp that year.

*With friends on a sunny Nebraska day. Back row, left to right, Sondra Johnson, **Norris** peeking in, **Margie;** front row, Judy Johnson, and **Carole Ann.***

A wonderful memory is watching lightning bugs on a warm summer evening. They looked like stars falling from the night sky or like twinkling Christmas lights. Lightning bugs, or fireflies, light up at dusk to attract mates or prey. Norris caught lightning bugs and put them in a mason jar. Carole and I recall catching fireflies and removing the glowing lights so we could put them on our fingers and pretend they were bright shiny rings.

I was discussing this memory with my friend, Michelle, from Illinois, who also remembers the fun of lightning bug rings. It is ironic that we both, living hundreds of miles apart, have the same fond memories about lightning bugs. Are fantasies of shiny baubles and rings in little girls' genes?

One Sunday during the summer, my friend, Ann, and I rented a row boat at Medicine Creek Reservoir, 10 miles north of Cambridge. We referred to it as The Lake. Neither Ann nor I knew how to row a boat, but, being teenagers, we could do anything. We sat down in the row boat, each of us grasped an oar, and were merrily paddling away with no coordination in our strokes. The lake current kept taking us farther and farther from the shore. Ann and I soon realized we were in the middle of the lake just going around in circles. Now, we were panicky. Norris was in a motor boat water skiing with his friends. He finally saw Ann and me sitting in the row boat in the middle of the lake. I'm sure Norris realized he would be in big trouble if he did not help us. My brother took his time but finally rescued us. In retrospect, I imagine my brother and his friends would not let us ride in their boat, so Ann and I got our own boat out of sheer spite.

Medicine Creek Reservoir, created by the building of the Medicine Creek Dam, was officially named Harry Strunk Lake. Harry D. Strunk was the publisher of the McCook Gazette newspaper. After the flood of 1935 he began a long battle, aggressively lobbying for the development of a flood-control program. Twelve years later, after the 1947 Medicine Creek flood, a dam was built to control flooding in the area.

Highlights of summer were the fairs. My first ride on a Ferris wheel was at the County Fair in Beaver City. I rode the Ferris wheel with some friends, and I upchucked after getting off the ride. Good impression. Carnival rides are not high on my list of fun things to do, but the rest of the carnival was so exciting. I remember the games and a carny shouting at my friends and me to come play their games. I did not have a great deal of spending money, so I had to enjoy the atmosphere of the carnival rather than spend money. The carnival food smelled delicious. I did indulge and bought some cotton candy.

I went to the State Fair in Lincoln with my brother, Bob, and his wife, Norma. I was astounded by the size of the Nebraska State Fair. Bob, Norma, and I went to the stock car races. The race was very noisy and went on *forever!* After the race, Bob asked Norma to see what brand of tires were on the winning car. He thought the winning car would have a long-wearing brand of tires. Norma was tiny and squeezed through the crowd. She discovered the winning race car used Firestone tires.

Our family did not take many family vacations when I was a kid because my dad was busy with farm work in the summer. We did visit relatives in Boulder, Colorado, and friends in Loveland, Colorado, on a few occasions.

When traveling, my brother, Norris, my sister, Carole, and I played the ABC game along the way. The object of the game is to find all the letters of the alphabet in order on signs and billboards. A player would start by finding "a" in a word. As you announced your letter, you had to say the word it was in. On to the letter "b" and the whole alphabet. It was a competitive game as each child searched for his/her own letters. First one to "z" won the game. "Q" was a hard letter, so we were always looking for the Quaker State Oil signs. "X" and "z" were tough letters

A family snowball fight in the Rocky Mountains: left to right, **Carole Ann, Mom, Margie, Norris, and Dad.**

to find. This was before interstates and freeways, so the roads were filled with signs and billboards. The highways also went through towns and cities.

I do remember the first real vacation, a trip to Estes Park, Colorado. I was shocked to see snow in the mountains because it was summer. I recall the winding Trail Ridge Road leading to Estes Park. The road was so beautiful, with craggy cliffs lining the route and a mountain stream gurgling alongside the road. Estes Park is in the heart of the Rocky Mountains. This trip was the first time I had ever stayed in a motel. When paying the bill at the motel, my father was quoted as saying, "I just wanted to sleep here, not buy it." Of course, he was smiling and had a twinkle in his eyes.

When I was about 10, I spent my summer vacation in Rock River, a small town in Wyoming, with Aunt Isabelle and Uncle Dale. They owned a gas station and a motel. I am sure I was invited so I could help baby-sit their son, David Joe. I do not remember the baby-sitting, but I

Dad, Margie, and Norris on Trail Ridge Road on the way to Estes Park.

had a grand time. I got Cokes from the pop (midwestern name for a soda) machine at the gas station. I played in the old stagecoach by the

Margie in her cowgirl outfit with Uncle Dale.

gas station. My aunt and uncle bought me a pair of cowboy boots and a western outfit. We went to Cheyenne for Cheyenne Frontier Days. My aunt and uncle took me to Thermopolis to sit in the hot springs and to Teton National Park. Do you think I may have been a little bit spoiled that summer? Loved it!

*Cowgirl **Margie** with Uncle Dale's gas station in the background.*

I also met a boy named Johnnie that summer. My parents came to Wyoming to pick me up at the end of the summer, and, when they arrived, I was so excited about being asked to go to a dance with Johnnie that I burst into the room and went straight to my aunt to ask if I could go to the dance. Nice greeting after not seeing my parents all summer. I was in no hurry to go back to the farm.

After spending the summer in Wyoming, I read several books about horses: "My Friend Flicka," "Thunderhead," and "Green Grass of Wyoming" by Mary O'Hara. The series was set in Wyoming and that made them even more fun to read.

That summer in Wyoming is very memorable. I was away from my familiar surroundings, I felt very mature, and I loved being the center of attention. I was in awe of all the mountains.

***Margie** with cousin David Joe.*

134

Smith Holidays

A Mushy Valentine, Easter Dresses, Decoration Day, and Oyster Stew at Christmas

New Year's Eve was the end of the Christmas season for me. It was time to return to school, see my friends, and talk about our great Christmas.

The only Valentine's Day I recall is the year I received a very *mushy* valentine from my boyfriend in junior high. When our class had its 50th class reunion, I mentioned to Howard that I had found the Valentine. He said he remembered giving it to me. Memories ....

St. Patrick's Day was celebrated by wearing green, and we did pinch people who did not wear green. In high school, we were too cool to let the green show. At that time, men's Hanes underwear had a green and orange string, so all of the boys of course wanted to show the girls their green. The girls had to be a little subtle when having green in some unmentionable places.

Easter was a great holiday when I was a kid. Part of the Easter celebration was the ending of a long cold winter. It was ditching the old winter coats and sweaters for the thrill of sporting new spring clothing. My mother made my sister and me new spring dresses. We got new hats and, sometimes, a new pair of dress shoes. We wore the new outfit to church on Easter Sunday. After church services, we enjoyed a big Easter Dinner: ham, scalloped potatoes, and yummy desserts.

When I was a teenager, the MYF went to the lake for a beautiful Easter Sunrise Service. After the service, we went back to the church for hot chocolate and hot cross buns. (A hot cross bun is a spiced sweet bun with a cross of frosting on top. It was traditionally eaten on Good Friday to signify the end of Lent.)

A tradition on Mother's Day when I was growing up was mothers wearing corsages to church. If her mother was alive, the flowers in the corsage were red, and, if their mother was no longer living, the corsage had white

Carole Ann and *Margie Lou* with their new Easter clothes.

flowers. My grandmother was living, so my mother always wore a beautiful red corsage.

Memorial Day was a holiday the family observed, but we called it by its former name, Decoration Day. My parents decorated relative's graves scattered around the Cambridge Cemetery with bouquets of flowers. Flags were placed on the graves of veterans. The family attended the Memorial Day service at the Cambridge Cemetery, which included posting the flag, prayer by a local minister, playing of taps, reading the names of those Cambridge men who died in war, the Gettysburg Address recited by a graduating senior, and a 21-gun salute by a Color Guard made up of Cambridge men who had served in the military. My brother, Bob, was part of the Color Guard. I still picture in my mind the sights, sounds, and precision of the twenty-one-gun salute. It was a very moving ceremony. Our family usually had a picnic with relatives from out of town on Memorial Day.

There was always a discussion about whether the peony plants would bloom by Memorial Day as peonies were the preferred flower to place on the graves. I was always amazed the peony plants seemed to know and opened up with their beautiful flowers on Memorial Day morning.

Norris lit firecrackers under my bedroom window early on the Fourth of July and scared me to death. I also had my share of firecrackers and sparklers. The Fourth wasn't a huge celebration as the families we knew were harvesting wheat around the Fourth of July. A memory I have is taking lunch to my dad and brothers in the wheat field. My mom would fix lunch, and we ate it in the wheat field with my dad.

Our family had a large picnic on Labor Day. My mother said that, since I was born on Labor Day, she got out of cooking for the holiday picnic. I like to think that she was also excited about having a beautiful baby daughter. My birthday was always close to Labor Day, so two holidays were celebrated. School started right after Labor Day, making it a special day, because I got to go back to school.

The memory I have of Veteran's Day is seeing people wearing red crepe paper poppies in honor of servicemen and women. Again, we used the original name, "Armistice Day," the anniversary of the end of World War I. The American Legion passed out poppies to raise funds for veterans.

One thing I remember about Thanksgiving as a child was helping my mother make cranberry sauce. She attached the old metal grinder to the edge of the counter, popped the cranberries into the hopper, and I turned the crank to grind up the cranberries. She also roasted a turkey stuffed with dressing and baked delicious pumpkin pies. Mom made the whipped cream for the pumpkin pie using a hand eggbeater. She turned the handle on that eggbeater *so* fast that her hand was just a blur.

I loved the Christmas season. I remember my dad bringing home a Christmas tree. My mother would get the box of *well used* Christmas decorations out of the closet. The first thing was testing the strings of lights. If one light on the string of lights went out, the whole set was out, so it was a real challenge to get the set working; it was like the scene in the movie, "A Christmas Story." After the kids put decorations on the tree, Dad carefully placed the angel on top of the tree. I fondly remember getting to decorate the tree with "icicles" (tinsel). I would start by carefully placing the icicles one at a time on a tree branch. Before long, it became a game of my brother and I throwing the icicles higher and higher. Then we were laughing and throwing bunches of icicles at the tree. Soon the box of icicles was empty, and the fun was over. Our tree was not always neatly decorated, but I thought it was gorgeous.

Our church had a Christmas program every year. To me, the highlight of the Christmas program was a brown bag of Christmas goodies that Santa passed out. It was filled with candy, peanuts, and my favorite, a fresh juicy orange. I'm sure in the middle of rural Nebraska, during the dead of winter, fresh oranges were quite rare. I was overwhelmed by the orange in my bag of goodies. It's curious how times change; now I have an orange tree in my backyard.

I have a vivid memory of one Christmas morning when I was very young. My mother opened the double doors to the living room, and I stood in utter amazement looking at the beautiful Christmas tree. The lights were dazzling, all the decorations were sparkling in the light, and under the tree were wrapped Christmas presents. I still remember staring at the magnificent sight and feeling as though I was in a dream.

Oyster stew on Christmas Eve was a tradition at our house. My mother added chili to the menu because some of the kids did not like the oysters. I remember my dad coming home from the grocery with one or two white cardboard cartons of fresh oysters. Bob thought Dad was a little chintzy with the oysters. Bob arrived on Christmas Eve with two more boxes of oysters for the oyster stew. Amazing – having fresh oysters in the middle of the United States so far from the ocean. After some research, I found that oyster stew on Christmas Eve is a very common tradition, especially among the families of Irish decent. A Catholic religious practice in Ireland was to abstain from eating meat on Christmas Eve. Oysters were readily available along the East Coast. Actually, Native Americans had been harvesting oysters for years. The tradition of oyster stew on Christmas Eve continued as families moved west.

When I was quite young, I recall seeing Santa Clause in Cambridge. On a December Saturday afternoon, the end of Main Street was blocked off, and Santa was giving out candy. My memory is standing in the middle of the street with my dad waiting to see Santa Claus. Carole remembers Cambridge having a drawing for prizes on Main Street every Saturday in December. I just remember seeing Santa Claus.

As kids, we each got one gift for Christmas. Mom had a way of knowing what we wanted. I was always snooping around to find my gift before Christmas. One year, I found mine, a new case for my clarinet. What a disappointment on Christmas morning; I had seen the one thing I was getting, so no surprise. The next year, I did not try to find my Christmas present.

I began wondering recently: How did my mother find all of the items the kids wanted for Christmas? Instead of Black Friday, companies published Christmas catalogs – we called them wish books – each fall. Those catalogues were filled with a multitude of things. I realize my mother searched the Sears and Roebuck and Montgomery Ward catalogs, found each and every gift, filled out an order form in the back of the catalogs. She mailed the order forms along with a check to Sears and Montgomery Ward. There were no credit cards to pay the bill. The catalog companies filled the orders, wrapped each item in brown paper, and shipped them to the Cambridge post office. The items were then delivered to our house by the mailman. Just think of this as the precursor of Amazon.com. Amazon.com is just the up-to-date version of mail-order catalogs.

AND we were modern because we recycled. All of the old catalogs were put in the outhouse. Just use your imagination on that one.

School Days

One-Room School, Box Socials, Cheerleading, and 1950s Style

I attended a country school in first and second grade. It had one teacher for eight grades. In third grade, I started school at Cambridge Elementary School. Grade school and junior high were in the same building. The high school, Cambridge High, was adjacent to the elementary school. The whole school shared the same cafeteria, located in the elementary school.

When I was a child, school started after Labor Day, ended around the middle of May, and included at least a week vacation at Christmas. I remember getting a new pair of shoes each year before going back to school. I usually got saddle oxfords, but one year it was penny loafers.

I learned to read using readers. The stories had the characters Dick, Jane, and little sister Sally. Spot the dog and Puff the cat were in the stories. The basal readers published

Dick and Jane book.
Courtesy of Cambridge Museum.

by Scott Foresman were used in public schools from the 1930s through the 1970s. The Dick and Jane collections were look and say readers. They were sight word based and did not use phonics. By repetition, using pictures for clues, first-grade students were taught to read.

In school, arithmetic was learning addition, subtraction, and multiplication facts. The arithmetic book also had a lot of story problems. I remember arithmetic flashcard drills. I also played a game called "Climb the Ladder" using arithmetic flashcards. I laid ten flashcards on the floor horizontally, like the rungs of a

Potbellied stove, Sunny Hillside School. Unlike this replacement, the stove I remember had a flat top and would not have been close to a student chair.

Sunny Hillside School in 1934.

142

ladder. The object of the game was to give the correct answers as I stepped up the ladder. If I got a fact wrong, I fell off the ladder and started over again.

My arithmetic lessons were rote memorization of number facts, learning the traditional operations of addition, subtraction, multiplication, and division. Learning and performing the operations, rather than understanding the process, were emphasized.

Sunny Hillside School was built in 1885 and served as a one-room school house for 75 years. It was a country school two and one-half miles southeast of Cambridge. The school sat on a small hill. This fact may have contributed to its name. Sunny Hillside was an eight-grade school with one teacher. The schoolhouse had one large room accommodating all eight grades. It had a small entrance that also served

1912: Charles Smith attends Sunny Hillside.
*Back row, left to right: Hazel Smith, **Charles Smith**, Bessie Hardin, and Esther Sayer;*
second row: Albert Gutzman, Della Smith, Edna Sayer, Sadie Sayer, Clarence Gutzman,
and Charles Hardin; front row: Lee Tyson, Justin Hollingsworth, Guy Tyson, Johnnie
Sayer, and unidentified girl.

as a coat room. Student lunch pails, as well as their coats and boots, were kept in the coatroom. In the schoolroom, desks were lined up in

Sunny Hillside School
1913-1914

Back row left to right: Ethel Paxton
Charles Smith,Frank Hicks, Bertha
Luctavish (Teacher), Esther Sayer Haggert
Hazel Smith Kelly, Robert Hicks,
 Middle row: Frank Paxton,Edna Sayer Fatt
Della Smith Deterding, Bertha Hicks Milla
Mabel Sayer Younker, Mary Hicks Oxford,
Alice Thuman Chitwood,Johnnie Sayer,
 Front row: Clarence Gutzman, Albert
Gutzman,Johnnie Brown,Kenneth Hicks,
Cecil Lohmeyer, Sadie Sayer Graf,Lee
Tyson,Lawrence Brown and Guy Tyson.
                    Respectfully submitted,
                    Sadie Graf

rows, and the students were seated according to grade. There was a round potbellied stove in the back of the room for heating the schoolroom. In the winter, students would set their containers of soup on top of the stove to keep their soup warm.

About 350 students attended Sunny Hillside School. Two generations of many families went to school there. The Smiths, Gutzmans, Sayers, Estergards, and Browns are some of the Cambridge families having two generations attend Sunny Hillside. My father, Charles Smith, and four of his siblings enrolled in Sunny Hillside School in 1908.

My older brothers and sisters and Norma Johnson (Bob's wife) attended Sunny Hillside School, 1937-38.
*Left to right: back row, Bob Cady; second row from back, Charles Gutzman, **Bud Smith**, **Bob Smith**, Bonnie Smith (cousin), Joy Olson, unidentified girl, Patty Brown; third row from back, unidentified girl, Betty Cady (with dark hair), unidentified girl (looking down), unidentified girl (also looking down); fourth row from back, Charles Tyson, Paul Johnson, **Duane Smith**, Betty Rickets, **Joyce Smith**, Elaine Smith (cousin), **Joan Smith**, **Norma Johnson** (looking over Joan Smith's shoulder), and Reba Olson.*

In September of 1945, I started school at Sunny Hillside. Six of my brothers and sisters had preceded me in attending Sunny Hillside. Norris was in second grade. There was no kindergarten, so I started my schooling in first grade. My teacher was my aunt, Dorothy (Perdue) Moore. The school had about 18 students in grades one through eight. There were four students in

Geography text at Sunny Hillside School.

my first-grade class, two girls and two boys. The first graders sat together. Quite often the older students helped the younger students with their school lessons. I remember sitting by the left back window

Miss Doris tenBensel (who would later marry a local farmer named Fletcher).

in first grade. Not sure why I remember that. Country school did not have hot lunch, so I carried a lunch pail to school. I took sandwiches and sometimes a thermos with hot soup. As a treat, occasionally my mom would pack chocolate sandwiches (like Nutella on bread), and I was the envy of my fellow students on those days. We got drinking water by pumping it from the pump in front of the school. A cup was fastened to the pump by a curved wire, and we all drank water using the same tin cup.

I had the same classmates in second grade: Dalwin Sayer, Jimmy Foster, and Jackie Sayer. Miss tenBensel was our teacher at Sunny Hillside in 1946-47. Sunny Hillside School was straight south of our farm. I walked across the neighbor's cornfield and pasture with my brother to get to and from school. Some afternoons, I walked home with a friend and took the dirt road on my way home. My friend, Jackie,

Margie's school picture for third grade.

lived to the east of the school and another friend, Sondra, lived to the west, so it was a longer walk in either direction. One day, while walking home from school by myself across the neighbor's pasture, I saw their bull. I taunted that bull, and he began chasing me. I took off running like a bat out of hell and rolled under the fence to get away from him. I was scared to death and still remember how fast I ran that day.

Sunny Hillside School had no playground equipment, so the students played games at recess: Red Rover, Simon Says, Pom-Pom Pull Away, Kick the Can, Hide and Seek, Mother May I, Red Light – Green Light, Hopscotch, and marbles.

Red Rover was a rather rough game. I am surprised we did not have a rash of broken arms. The game consisted of two teams holding hands and facing each other. The game starts when the first team shouts, "Red rover, red rover, send (player on the opposite team) right over." That player runs and tries to break through the opponent's line. If the runner fails, he joins the opposing team. If successful, he gets to choose two students to join his team. The winner is the team with the most players at the end of the game.

My favorite game was Simon Says. A much calmer game using brains instead of brawn. The leader of the game, Simon, would tell players what to do: take two steps backward, for example, or touch your nose. However, you obeyed the direction only if it began with, "Simon says." If Simon just said, "Touch your nose," then you did not obey. Those who did touch their nose were out. The last person in the games wins and is the new leader.

At our country school there were two outhouses, boys and girls. On the school grounds, there was also a cave to use in the event of storms. Some of the older girls at school set up a little beauty shop in the cave, and they would curl or braid my hair at recess. Apparently, we were unaware of head lice. I remember Marianne Sayer braiding my hair.

Sunny Hillside – 1943-44 – Teacher, Betty Summers.
*Back row, left to right, Carl Johnson, Paul Johnson, **Duane Smith**, Glenn Brooks, Charles Tyson, Betty Rickets, Reba Olson, **Joyce Smith, Joan Smith**; front row, unidentified boy, Leonard Sayer, unidentified boy, Connie Sayer, Marianne Sayer, Ardis Gutzman, and Sharon Johnson.*

In grade school, music was part of our curriculum. We sang and learned to read music. We had music books in our desks. The books had some pages with words to a familiar song, while other pages had music written with the lyrics. A part of the music class I fondly remember is when the Miss tenBensel used her music chalkboard staff writer. It was a wire contraption attached to a wooden handle. She put five pieces of chalk in the gizmo, grabbed the handle, and glided it across the chalkboard, and there magically was a musical staff. Miss tenBensel added the treble clef, notes, sharps, flats, and I learned to read music.

I remember a boy from my Sunny Hillside School days. He may have been what we now call a bully. He was a grade ahead of me, and I was a little frightened of him. One day, he had just sharpened his pencil, and, as he was returning to his seat, he gouged me in the cheek with his pencil. I had that scar for years. I just looked in the mirror to see if it is still there, but I can't distinguish the scar from all the wrinkles.

The small step-up is the stage.

The stage and box socials at Sunny Hillside are vivid memories. Box socials were an annual event at Sunny Hillside. In retrospect, I assume they were a way of making extra money for the school. The mothers packed a lunch for two in a fancy box that was auctioned to the highest bidder. Our school had a stage at the front of the schoolroom. The stage was raised up one step. I remember standing nervously on that stage as my box was being auctioned. The gentleman, boy, who got my box lunch would get to sit with me and eat the lunch. I was quite young, so I am sure the person buying my box lunch only wanted my mother's great cooking. Students also performed in a Christmas program on that stage. That stage seemed so intimidating as a child. When visiting it as an adult, it seemed extremely small.

Sunny Hillside Country School closed in the spring of 1947. I was the last of the Smiths to attend Sunny Hillside. At the start of my third-grade year, Norris and I transferred to what we called town school in Cambridge.

In 1964, the Sunny Hillside school building was moved from its hill in the country to the city park in Cambridge. It was opened as Sunny Hillside Museum. Quoting from a June 4, 1964, article in the Cambridge Clarion, "Although no longer on a hill, it's still in a good location, as Sunny Hillside school house will be preserved for posterity at Cambridge roadside park."

Norris and I had the same reaction when revisiting the Sunny Hillside School at the park in Cambridge. The school house seemed so small.

Marje visiting Sunny Hillside Museum in 2017.

After a log school, a sod school, and a frame school, the first brick school house in Cambridge was built in 1888. By 1910, the school was crowded, and a new larger brick school building was built. Until 1926 grades 1-12 were housed in that school building. I attended grade school and junior high in the 1910 brick school house from 1947-1954.

On my first day in town school, I found the large school building somewhat overwhelming. There were so many rooms in the school. I was one of the new kids in school, as most of my classmates had been together since first grade. I gradually settled into my larger third-grade class. I remember many of the lessons taught in third grade; I had already learned them in country school. In country school, with so many grades together, lessons were combined. After a short adjustment time, I enjoyed town school. I thought I had the greatest teacher. There were

Cambridge Elementary School.
Photo courtesy of Cambridge Public School.

so many girls my age to hang out with. Town school had a lunch room that served hot lunches, so I did not have to take my lunch pail.

Most days, my dad drove us to school in town – well, almost to school. He dropped Norris, Carole, and me off and made us walk a few blocks to school. He came to town every morning to deliver milk and let us out of the car between the two grocery stores where he delivered milk. Of course, I complained about having to walk to school. "Don't want to spoil you!" my dad quipped.

There was a bunch of playground equipment at Cambridge Elementary. The swings and the merry-go-round were my favorite. When I was in fifth and sixth grade, I played on the giants. I hung onto a bar connected to a high pole with a chain, and the top of the pole rotated. I would hang onto the bar, run fast, pull up my feet, and sail through the air. *Wow, so much fun!* Giants would not be allowed on playgrounds today because they would be considered *dangerous*.

Another recess amusement was jumping rope. Classmates took turns swinging a long rope. Jumping rope was considered a girl's game. The boys engaged in what they perceived as more masculine endeavors: teasing and chasing girls. As grade school girls, we had many games using jump ropes: running in while the rope was turning, counting the number of jumps before a missed jump, jumping hot peppers (very fast),

1951 – Recess at Cambridge Elementary School: left to right, Sandra Stanton, Sandra Danfield, Jackie Sayer, Vivian Johnson, **Margie Smith.**

jumping doubles, and chanting rhymes while jumping the rope.

A fun jump rope rhyme was: "Cinderella dressed in yellow, went downstairs to kiss her fellow (had to touch the ground while saying this). How many times did he kiss her? 1! 2! 3!" Counting continued until a miss.

My favorite teacher in grade school was my third-grade teacher, Mrs. McLane. I remember her as being kind, having a great sense of humor, and being very caring. She recalled me saying, "I never want to be a teacher because I don't want anyone not to like me." (I know, double negatives.)

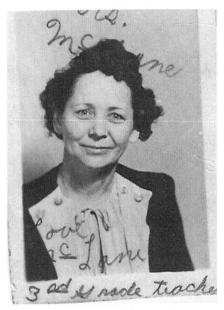

Mrs. McLane.

My fourth-grade teacher was Mrs. McReynolds. After having such a kind teacher in third grade, Mrs. McReynolds seemed harsh. I don't remember Mrs. McReynolds' exact comments, but they must have made an impression on me, because after I grew up, I realized that she was prejudiced. At the time, I did not even understand the concept of being prejudiced.

My fifth-grade teacher, Mrs. Bose, was also a great teacher. As a student, I always marveled at how much Mrs. Bose knew about science and geography. She showed the class so many interesting and exciting places on her large, pull-down map.

A favorite day in grade school was going on a field trip to McCook to attend the Shrine Circus. The circus was held indoors at the McCook Auditorium. The circus ring was so close to the audience that students could almost reach out and touch the animals. My dad took a carload of eager students for several years. I especially liked sitting in the balcony and watching the show. I usually had enough money to buy a treat or trinket. The big pink ball of cotton candy was my favorite treat at the circus. I loved the sugary taste as it melted in my mouth. I was not tempted by a lizard that changed colors that the circus venders were hawking.

My fifth-grade teacher, Mrs. Bose.
Photo Courtesy of Cambridge Museum.

In May, before school was dismissed for the summer, Cambridge Elementary School had Field Day. It was a day filled with all kinds of sporting events and races. My favorite events were the gunny sack race, three-legged race, and the slipper kick. Kids in the gunny sack race had to run fast with the restraint of being inside a gunny sack and trying not to fall. My friend, Jackie, and I became quite proficient in the three-legged race. We tied two adjoining legs together with a scarf and then ran as a couple with three legs. We practiced at recesses before field day. Once we got coordinated, it went well; if not, we were both flat on our faces. But, my all-time favorite was the slipper kick. I stood on a line with my shoe loose on my foot. On a signal, I kicked my shoe as far as possible. The winner of the slipper kick was the student who kicked her shoe the greatest distance. Saddle oxfords could really sail through the air if kicked correctly. I do not remember if I won the slipper kick contest; I only remember watching my shoe slowly sailing through the air after I kicked it.

When my older sisters, Joyce and Joan, were seniors in high school they drove us to and from school. There were no school buses to ride. One of my memories of grade school is waiting ... and waiting ... on the playground for my twin sisters to pick me up after school so I could go home. My sisters were out driving around with their friends, oblivious to my sitting on a playground swing and waiting endlessly. I'm sure it did not happen as often as I remember it, but it is a vivid memory. Everyone else was gone ... and I was there ... by myself ... waiting.

My sixth-grade teacher, Miss Anderbery.

In sixth-grade, my class moved *upstairs*. It was a self-contained classroom, but we sixth-graders had moved up! My sixth-grade teacher was a young teacher, Miss Anderbery. Most of my teachers had been older, so I thought she was young and beautiful.

There was a teacher's room across from our sixth-grade class room. One day, I went on an errand to the teacher's room. There I saw this strange thing called a hectograph. It was used to make copies. A dye-impregnated master was laid onto a flat gelatin-like surface. As the dye from the master soaked into the gelatin, sheets of paper were laid on the surface to make copies. I remember touching the gelatin. It was soft and slimy to the touch and felt so creepy.

In seventh grade, my class made the grand move to junior high – across the hall. Junior high consisted of one regular-sized classroom and another very large room used as a classroom and library. The larger room had enough seats for the whole junior high to have study hall. I remember a very large dictionary sitting on a stand and a globe in the library area. Those two items clearly stand out in my memory of junior high. Both rooms had pull-down maps and lots of blackboards. Students went through a small hall to change classes.

The school lunch room was across the hall from our junior high classrooms. When I was in the eighth grade, I worked during my lunch time in the school cafeteria. I collected dirty dishes, restocked the milk, and loaded dishes to be washed. The job paid for my lunch and, as an added bonus, I could be late for afternoon classes.

Quoting from the "Cambridge Centennial Book" about the lunch program, "The service of the hot lunch program in Cambridge had its beginnings in 1946. Through the efforts of the PTA, two upstairs rooms of the junior high were converted to a cafeteria. Mrs. Glenn Moore (my aunt, Dorothy), PTA president then, recalls how she and Grace Newcomb, Cambridge school librarian, scoured the local auction sales in search of chairs, tables, pots, pans, and other furnishings. Supplies were so meager at the beginning that each child had to bring his own plate and silverware to leave in the lunch room for day-to-day use."

Pep Club and cheerleading were the only sports for girls. The junior high boys had a football and a basketball team. The girls sat on the

sidelines yelling, jumping, and cheering for the team. Junior high pep club members wore white blouses and navy circle skirts. As a cheerleader, I wore navy tights so my undies wouldn't show as I twirled.

Junior High cheerleaders.

My first boyfriend was Howard. We were in junior high. On Saturday nights, I would meet him in front of a movie theatre and go to the movie with him. When the movie was over, Howard and I walked to the drugstore and had a Coke. After the *date*, I went home with my dad. This all happened on Main Street in Cambridge. It was more fun than it sounds. My first kiss was at the Ritz Theatre on a Saturday night.

While I was in junior high school, I visited Joyce and Joan in their dorm room at Kearney State Teachers College. The following year, they secured jobs as secretaries and moved to Lincoln. They had an apartment in downtown Lincoln near the Nebraska State Capital. I remember visiting Joyce

The 1953 Junior High Pep Club.
I took this picture.

and Joan at their apartment in Lincoln during the summer. Before we went to bed, we ate a large watermelon. In the middle of the night, I was afraid to get up and go to the bathroom because I might step on big black water bugs that came out in the dark. (I called them cockroaches.) By morning, I had to go, and I nearly wet my pants. My bladder still aches thinking of that night.

The next summer, my sisters and their roommates rented a house in Lincoln. In their house was this strange-looking, round-screen television. I do not remember the show, but I stared in wonder at the picture on the television set.

Girls haven't changed; we also thought the whole world was looking at and judging us. Our family delivered milk before going to school. I had to walk across the highway carrying a milk carrier with bottles of milk for the local restaurant each morning while my dad delivered milk to the grocery store. At the time, this was SO embarrassing.

Even in my day we complained about our hair. Always! I don't remember any bad haircuts, although I'm sure I complained about them. What I do remember are the home permanents that my mother gave me. Home permanents always seemed to turn out frizzy, and I grumbled for days.

An embarrassing time in junior high was after I broke my arm skating. Another boy also came back to school after Christmas vacation sporting a sling holding a broken arm. I remember being uncomfortable that he and I had broken arms in common. After all the attention I had received from my family after breaking my arm, I was not so special in school because there were two students with broken arms. I was just another kid with a broken arm. Teenage problems.

My teachers in junior high were: Mrs. Phelps, math teacher and principal; Mrs. Dobbie, English; Mr. Michael, social studies; and Miss Grice, music. I do remember Mr. Michael giving students a swat on the behind if we were talking while changing classes, a no-no in schools today.

I connect my memories of high school years to the great 1950s. As a high school student, I embraced many of the styles, music, and fads of the 50s. These are my memories of that time.

The 1950s are legendary. Rock 'n' roll was born in the 1950s. Our parents hated it and thought it was just a fad. (Remind you of another music genre?) Rock and Roll was featured in the movie "Blackboard Jungle" and was further popularized by Bill Haley and the Comets. "Rock Around the Clock" was considered to be the first commercial success for Rock and Roll. The King of Rock and Roll, Elvis Presley, was an icon of the time with "Jail House Rock," "Hound Dog," and "Blue Suede Shoes" to name a few. Other popular songs were: "Rock Around the Clock," "Blueberry Hill," "Yellow Rose of Texas," "Sixteen Tons," and "Wake Up Little Susie."

I heard the popular songs, saw rock 'n' roll stars perform, and watched teenage couples dancing to all the popular songs on the TV show, "American Bandstand."

My favorite singing group of the 50s changed quite often depending on what was popular that week. I liked rock 'n' roll, but I also liked the love songs of the time, "Secret Love" by Doris Day, "Sincerely" by the McGuire Sisters, and "If I Loved You" from the movie "Carousel." I listened to music on the family radio, "American Bandstand," or a jukebox.

My granddaughter, Madison, in a typical '50s outfit: poodle skirt, letter sweater, saddle oxfords, and bobby socks.

I did not have a record collection, a transistor radio, a tape collection, CDs, or a playlist on an iPod or phone. I had a few 45s that I played on my sister's little red record player. SO deprived! I was not an Elvis Presley fan or one of those screaming teenage girls who fainted when they saw or heard Elvis.

***Marje**, with rolled up jeans and penny loafers.*

Some of the fads during my youth were bullet boxes for purses, dog tags for bracelets, DA haircuts (called duck *tails* in my circle of friends), poodle skirts, big fluffy crinoline underskirts (we called them can-cans), letter sweaters, neckerchiefs (a small square scarf worn around the neck), saddle oxfords, penny loafers, bobby socks, and charm bracelets. Coonskin caps were popular, but I didn't see many of those in Cambridge. I remember buying a bullet box. I asked my friends and family to autograph my bullet box and carried it as purse.

Girls in the '50s wore midcalf straight skirts and matching sweaters and poodle skirts. I wore a can-can under my poodle skirt. I starched the can-can to make it fuller. I also wore jeans rolled up at the bottom. A summertime style was pedal pushers. My mother made me a pair of blue pedal pushers. Pedal pushers, popular with teenage girls in the 1950s, were calf-length pants. The name pedal pushers described trousers originally worn by cyclist to keep their pant legs out of the bicycle chain. Now they are called capris.

My bullet box purse.

Pants with a buckle in the back was a style when I was in high school. The style was popular with teenage girls, but teachers and parents were not so thrilled about the pants with buckles in the back. When sitting down, the buckle would scratch desks and chairs. Mom did not like the style because the buckle caught on our couch upholstery fabric.

In college, stuffing students into telephone booths or Volkswagen Bugs as well as panty raids were popular. Hula Hoops made their debut in 1957. Carhops waited on customers at the drive-in restaurants. The first Pizza Hut opened in 1958 in Wichita, Kansas.

Things have changed. In the 1950s, "hippie" meant large hips, "far out" was a distance away, "grass" was mowed, "Coke" was a cold drink, "pot" was something you cooked in, a "trip" was going someplace, "thongs" were worn on your feet, "drugs" were pills bought in pharmacies, and "hang up" was something done on the phone.

Technology brought more changes: in my era, "hardware" was bought in hardware stores, "cloud" was visible in the sky, "swipe" was to steal something, "tweet" was a bird sound, "text" was a book for school, "spam" was canned meat, "tablet" was what we wrote in, "tag" was a kid's game, "stream" was a body of water, and "unlike" was not the same. Software, selfies, photobombing, and unfriending were not words.

When I was young, we didn't have credit cards, panty hose, contact lenses, dishwashers, air conditioners, portable hair dryers, permanent-press clothing, or computers. Smoking was fashionable.

By 1926, the student population of Cambridge had outgrown the 1910 brick school house. A new high school building was constructed and opened in 1927. In 1952, just before I entered high school, a new gymnasium, a music room, a vocational agricultural room, and dressing rooms were added to the 1927 brick high school. That same brick high school serves as the high school today.

I attended Cambridge High, beginning as a freshman in September of 1954 and graduated in May of 1958. The high school building seemed enormous after a junior high of only two classrooms. There were about 120 students in Cambridge High, and there were 33 students in my freshman class. Classrooms were on two levels. The high school had a library, a room full of typewriters for typing class, a science room, an auditorium, a music room, and a gymnasium with dressing rooms. I had my very own locker. We were really uptown!

With all the facilities, my high school education was pretty basic. For the one term paper I wrote in high school, I used an encyclopedia as my only source of information. I did not receive instruction on how to prepare or write a term paper. (Could be that I wasn't listening?) Consequently, when I wrote my freshman English term paper in college, I was at a loss. I did not read many of the classics. I do remember a unit on Shakespeare, taught by Mrs. Pope, but did not understand it.

(Still don't.) Also, at that time, foreign languages were not offered in most small high schools.

I liked English, geography, and history classes. For an English oral class book report, I remember choosing a book by Audie Murphy called "To Hell and Back." I chose the book *only* because you had to write the name of the book on the blackboard before you gave your book report. I thought it was so *brazen* to write the swearword "hell" on the blackboard.

In high school, I did not care for biology or algebra. Math wasn't my thing. I liked geometry better than algebra. Mr. Pope, the principal, taught all the math courses. He was an excellent teacher, but I only took the two required math courses.

Cambridge High School, 2017.

There were no hand-held calculators when I was in high school. Difficult math calculations were done using a slide rule. A slide rule is described as a mechanical analog computer. Three specially numbered bars were fixed together with a metal window used as a placeholder. The center bar slid back and forth. I never used one, but I remember being fascinated watching my older brother, Duane, use a slide rule when he was in college. I watched him slide the bar with tiny complex numbers up and down to find the answer for his projects. Perhaps if I had tried a little harder in math, I could have used and understood the functions of the slide rule.

One of my high school teachers was Mr. Potter. He was very tall, well dressed, and a bit conceited. I remember Mr. Potter wearing a brightly colored bow tie with his suit. He taught the science classes. Besides taking biology, which was required, I also took physics. In physics class, when Mr. Potter called on me, I blushed and turned red, even if I knew the answer. Perhaps he caught me talking or passing notes to my friends. Mr. Potter seemed pretty intimidating to me.

In high school, I took home economics, which we called "home ec." Mrs. Petefish was my home economics teacher. We learned about sewing, cooking, decorating, and personal finance. I made an apron for a sewing project. One day in home economics class, we cooked macaroni and cheese. It was thick, dry, and cooked in the oven. *I hated it*, but we always sat down at tables and ate our creations. That day I sat next to my friend, Judy Avery, who loved macaroni and cheese. Every time Mrs. Petefish looked the other way, I scooped some of my macaroni and cheese onto Judy's plate. I successfully got rid of all the macaroni and cheese on my plate by the time class was over.

In high school, our school colors were orange and black, and the school mascot was a Trojan (that was before it had a different meaning.) I was a cheerleader during football and basketball season. High school cheerleaders wore black skirts and orange letter sweaters, bobby sox, and of course, saddle oxfords.

1957 – High school cheerleaders, left to right, Vivian Johnson, Chris Berres, and **Marjorie Smith.**

I had cheerleading practice after school. As a cheerleader, I learned the words and actions to accompany the cheers. The cheerleading team practiced the cheers, jumping, spinning around, clapping, and yelling rah, rah, rah.

A cheer for the football team was, "First and ten – do it again." It took me a while to understand what a first and ten was in football. I am sure my brothers would be embarrassed that I did not know. They all played football for the Cambridge Trojans. Another favorite cheer for the football team was "John, John, he's our man, if he can't do it George can. George, George he's our man" … etc. (Put in the team member's names and repeat.)

The Smith family owned two musical instruments, a clarinet and a trombone. The boys played the trombone. I was not a trendsetter; I didn't want to break tradition, so being a girl, I chose to play the clarinet in the school band.

*Majorettes left to right: **Marjorie Smith**, Chris Berres, and Vivian Johnson, the drum major.*

I was a majorette in the marching band. The marching band performed a halftime show for all the home football games. Being in the marching band required getting to school an hour early, meeting at the football field, and practicing every morning during football season. I really hated to get up early. On game nights, I had to change into my short majorette uniform and white boots for the halftime show. In Nebraska, fall nights can be very cold. As majorettes, we were twirling, throwing, and catching cold metal batons. I remember goose bumps on my legs and having cold hands. Brrr! But I loved it.

In addition to performing for all the football home games, the high school band entered district marching competitions and marched in several parades. Majorettes not only had to keep in step but march high-stepping the

Marje Smith *and Paul Ellis initiated into the National Honor Society.*

whole parade. I started the parade strutting my stuff, but by the end of a long parade route, I marched with a little less bravado. The school bus rides, comradery with friends, and meeting band members from other towns are fond memories.

A highlight of being a member of the Cambridge High School marching band was Band Day at the University of Nebraska in Lincoln. Each year, Nebraska High School bands were invited to participate in Band Day. I participated in Band Day my junior year in high school. According to a post on the Nebraska State Bandmasters Association's website, "Participation was limited to 3,600 band members each year because that was the number of seats available in the north and south end zones." Prior to the University football game on Band Day, high

1958 – Band Day at University of Nebraska Stadium.
Photo courtesy of Nebraska State Bandmasters Association.

school bands were in a parade down "O" street in Lincoln. All the bands then performed in the stadium during the halftime of the University of Nebraska football game. It must have been a dazzling sight from the grandstand, seeing such a large number of colorfully uniformed bands performing in unison. Band members watched the football game from the "knothole" section. The knothole section consisted of wooden bleachers behind the end zones of the football field. Those were the cheap seats! The University of Nebraska stadium was much smaller and looked very different in the 1950s. This was before Bob Devaney arrived at the University of Nebraska in 1962 and turned Nebraska Cornhusker Football into a dynasty.

I participated in other extra-curricular activities in high school. I had small parts in a couple of plays in high school. I was not a great actress. I was photographer on the Annual Staff (yearbook) my senior year. As photographer, I took pictures with my Brownie Hawkeye Camera and collected random pictures of seniors to be printed in the school yearbook. Being photographer for the annual staff was so much fun and a lot of work.

Masonic Lodge.
Courtesy of Cambridge Museum.

When I was in high school, I belonged to Order of the Rainbow for Girls. This is an organization for girls sponsored by Masons. Rainbow meetings were held at the Masonic Lodge in Cambridge. We had dances in the basement of the Masonic Lodge. When I was a senior, I attended a state meeting of Order of the Rainbow for Girls in downtown Omaha at the Fontenelle Hotel. Such an adventure for a small-town girl. Omaha seemed so large, and the noise of all the traffic was a strange sound to my ears. I kept the hotel bill from that trip. Rooms at the Fontenelle Hotel were $5 per night.

My entry into the workforce was a summer job while in high school. I worked at the Cambridge Swimming Pool. My job was giving out baskets from behind the counter. Swimmers changed into their swim suits in the dressing rooms. I took the basket of clothes and gave each swimmer a number. When they were finished swimming, each customer would give me their number, and I would hand them their basket of clothes. Tough job! During my breaks, I went swimming. My boss was the high school football coach. My pay was a whole *35 cents* an hour. That was the going rate; not sure if any laws about minimum wage had been passed.

At Cambridge High, I had a small class, so we hung out together. Ann, Bonnie, Judy, Karol, and Vivian were my best friends in high school. I envied my friend Vivian. She was really built (Marilyn Monroe style), and all of the boys in school were gaga over her. Our favorite hangouts were Bellamy's and John's Drug Store. They both had soda fountains and tables for sitting while we drank our Cokes.

My friends and I congregated at Judy's and Ann's houses because they lived in town. My other friends lived in the country. We yakked, giggled, tried on clothes, experimented with makeup, and enjoyed other teenage girl pastimes.

My first dance in high school was a mixer held in the Cambridge

Wearing my new dress at the FFA Sweetheart Dance with Donnie Harding dressed in a coat and tie.

High gymnasium after the first football game of the season. The dances were also called "sock hops" because shoes were not allowed on the gym floor. The lights of the usually bright gym were turned down, a student played records on his/her record player, and we danced in our bobby socks. Unless a couple was going steady, there was little dancing for the first hour. The boys and girls stared at each other nervously across the room. Boys were in small groups talking, laughing, and trying to work up the nerve to ask a girl to dance. Finally, the boys approached and asked girls to dance. Of course, the dance was almost over. Fun times.

Another dance I remember was the Sadie Hawkins Day Dance. The dance is named after a character in the comic strip "Li'l Abner" created by Al Capp. On this day, the unmarried women of Dogpatch got to chase the bachelors and *marry up* their catches. The concept of the dance was … girls were empowered and did the asking. Girls asked boys to the dance and took the initiative and invited boys to dance. There was no sitting and staring on the sidelines; the girls were in charge. The Sadie Hawkins Day Dance was a lively dance. More fun times.

Sadie Hawkins Day seems passé now, but it was quite a progressive idea. In 1952, girls did not usually ask guys out.

I remember the FFA (Future Farmers of America) Sweetheart Dance because my mother let me purchase a dress at the local dress shop, Marline Togs, for the dance. I remember the dress as if I bought it yesterday. It was a red and white printed sleeveless sheath with a red cummerbund and a red jacket. My mother made most of my clothes, so I was thrilled to buy that dress. Donnie Harding and I were crowned King and Queen of the dance. It was an unforgettable night.

My friends and I had a lot of slumber parties. We spent our time during slumber parties calling boys, endlessly talking, walking the streets of Cambridge in our PJ's, and very little time sleeping. I brought my Brownie Hawkeye Camera and took lots of pictures. The boys seemed to have a party the same night as our slumber parties.

*Slumber Party. Behind the chair, Karol Taylor; front, left to right, **Marje Smith**, Ann Easter, and Vivian Johnson*

Coincidence? We gave them enough hints about our slumber parties … date, time, place.

I learned to drive a car on farm roads and in the small town of Cambridge. Cambridge had no stop lights or steep hills. I was anxious to get my driver's license after I turned 16. I could get my driver's license three days earlier if I took the test in McCook instead of our county seat of Beaver City, another very small, flat town. So, I took my driver's test in McCook. It was a large town about 25 miles west of Cambridge, and the town had numerous hills. As part of the driving test in McCook, the instructor had me drive up Norris Avenue. Of course, I encountered a red light on my way up the hill. I vividly remember the near panic of the predicament. Cars did not have automatic transmissions. To stop, I had to hold down the brake and clutch. Then to start up the hill, I had to slowly let out the clutch and push on the accelerator. I stood the chance of either starting with a jerk or killing the engine. I still feel the anxiety of the slow start up the hill. Somehow, I successfully mastered that hill and passed my test!

Many cars in the '50s did not have turn signals. To pass the test for a driver's license, you had to know the hand signals. For a left turn, a driver put the left arm straight out the window. A right turn signal was indicated by resting the left elbow on the window and pointing upward. Drivers also had to signal for a stop by angling the left arm down. This information was important to me because our car did not have turn signals. I remember using hand signals even if it was raining or snowing outside. I cranked the window down – no power windows – made my hand signal, then cranked it back up as soon as I could to keep the weather out.

After I got my driver's license, I did discover one steep hill in Cambridge. It is called Vinegar Knob. I do not know the origin of the name. I only know that it existed, and few people, except teenagers, used it. Vinegar Knob was a narrow dirt street in the north part of town and was rather secluded with tall trees on each side. Teenagers would dare each other to drive up and down Vinegar Knob. I remember my first drive down Vinegar Knob. My friends egged me on. I drove down the steep hill, my knuckles white from holding onto the steering wheel so tightly. I had the family car; I knew I would be in so much trouble if anything happened. At the bottom of the hill, my friends and I giggled, and I let out a sigh of relief. For a flatlander it was exciting. Nebraskans are sometimes referred to as flatlanders because of the flatness of our state.

I remember the Army-McCarthy hearings. People in the United States were fearful of communism. In 1950, Wisconsin Senator Joseph R. McCarthy, playing on the mistrust of communism in the American people, gave a speech alleging that hundreds of communists had infiltrated the federal government and federal agencies. McCarthy held anti-communist investigations and set about to expose "reds." He charged that the Army was soft on communism. In 1954, televised hearings into his charges against the Army were aired. The Army-McCarthy hearings lasted about two months.

As a 14-year-old, I remember watching some of the televised Army-McCarthy hearings on our one and only channel, Channel 13. I perceived McCarthy as being very aggressive, insulting witnesses, interrupting witnesses, and yelling at everyone. I remember watching as he covered the microphone with his hand and spoke to his attorney. Joseph McCarthy was not a great example for a young teenager to see. He did not display maturity and decorum as an elected official. McCarthy's charges proved to be unsubstantiated.

A chilling experience I vividly remember was in 1958. I was a senior in high school when mass murderer Charles Starkweather and his girlfriend, Caril Ann Fugate, went on a nine-day killing spree. In January of 1958, they murdered 10 people across the state of Nebraska. They murdered a teenage couple after stealing their car in outstate

Nebraska (outstate is away from Omaha or Lincoln). I remember being so scared. All school extracurricular activities were canceled, and kids went straight home from school while Starkweather was on the loose. According to Carole, my father bought a key so he could lock the doors of our house for the first time. Everyone was cautious and stayed close to home until the murdering couple was arrested.

When I entered high school, freshman initiation was an activity to endure. The seniors at school told the freshman what to wear on Initiation Day. I had to wear a swimsuit with a grass skirt.

*Freshman initiation: left to right, curious grade school kid, Judy Avery, Chuck Simon, and **Marje Smith**.*

The freshman students were taunted and given orders by the seniors that day (within reason). I also remember seniors writing on our skin with lipstick. Today it might be called hazing. Initiation Day was embarrassing, but humorous and friendly. We knew … someday we would be the *seniors!*

My first ride in a convertible was on a chilly Friday night in October 1957. At halftime during the homecoming football game,

***Marje** escorted by Ron Mousel and Ron Banzhaf.*

Bonnie, Ann, and I rode onto the Cambridge High School football field seated on the back of Stu Minnick's Chevrolet convertible. Stu Minnick owned the only convertible in the town of Cambridge. My friend, Bonnie, as queen, Ann and I as attendants were helped out of the convertible and escorted to center field by football players. I was excited to be elected an attendant at homecoming, but the biggest thrill was riding in that convertible. It left me with a lifelong love of convertibles.

My friend Bonnie on our Senior Sneak Day in Colorado.

My senior class participated in Sneak Day before graduation. Our class had made arrangements to charter a bus and picked a destination. We stole out of Cambridge in the middle of the night bound for Colorado. I am sure we had the help of our senior class advisor and our parents, but it was a secret. On our class Sneak Day, we went to The Cave of the Winds near Pikes Peak in Colorado and other attractions nearby. A chaperone, the football coach, went with us, and gave our class an ultimatum: if there was any drinking, we would go home immediately. I remember two things about the trip; I was astounded by the stalactites in the Cave of the Winds (they looked like giant colored icicles), and, I had my first taste of liquor. My friend, Jackie, (most unlikely girl to have done this) smuggled a bottle of wine in her suitcase. All the girls had a

*1957 Prom, left to right: Jackie Sayer, Stan Sexton, Chuck Simon, and **Marjorie Smith.***

172

taste of the wine and thought it was terrible but were excited that we had gotten away with drinking liquor. The irony was that the girls were assumed to be so innocent that we had no chaperone in our room. The boys were the troublemakers.

A major event in high school was the Junior-Senior Prom. The junior class picked the theme and decorated the venues for the prom. Our class theme as juniors was "Carousel," and our junior class decorated the school gym in the shape of a carousel, made from pastel-colored crepe paper streamers. The challenge was to keep the theme a secret from the seniors. After decorating most of Friday night and all day Saturday, we dressed in our formals and suits, had a dinner in the church dining hall (which we had also decorated), and then went to the gymnasium for the dance. I had only 25 classmates, so it was a huge undertaking. I remember all the decorating and then having so much fun dancing at the prom. Teenagers have so much stamina; I am exhausted thinking of that very long weekend.

I received a watch as a gift from my parents for high school graduation. Watches were typical graduation gifts. It was a beautiful Bulova watch, a great brand of watches at the time. My watch was silver with a diamond chip on each side of the watch face. It had a tiny diamond instead of the number 12. I loved that watch and wore it for many years.

I graduated from Cambridge High School on Wednesday, May 21, 1958. Commencement was held in the high school auditorium. Twenty-six seniors were in my graduating class. As my name was called, I walked up the steps and proudly walked across the stage to receive my diploma. Of course, I did not forget to reach up and move my tassel to the right.

On Memorial Day weekend of each year, Cambridge High has an Alumni Banquet. The alumni attending sit at tables with former classmates. My mother was at the banquet with some members of her

1922 graduating class. I remember sitting at a table for the class of 1958, as a new graduate that year. It was a strange feeling, being a graduate instead of a student. I spent 12 years of my young life as a student along with most of my classmates. We were moving on.

On September 1, 1958, I celebrated my 18th birthday. Two days later, a very memorable day, Mom, Dad, and Carole accompanied me on my journey to college. I was attending Nebraska Wesleyan, at Lincoln. Lincoln is a four-hour drive from Cambridge, and it was a *long*

way from home. Before checking in at Wesleyan, we went shopping in Lincoln. I bought a jade green matching skirt and sweater. Very fashionable! We also shopped for bedding for my dorm room. Then we drove through the city of Lincoln out to the Wesleyan campus.

Old Main at Nebraska Wesleyan University in Lincoln.

My dad, Mom, Carole, and I carried my meager belongings up two flights of stairs in Johnson Hall to my dorm room. I was excited, but sad and apprehensive, as I watched my parents and little sister walk down the hall … leaving me alone in my dorm room. I didn't know anyone at Wesleyan, not even my roommate.

I met my roommate Judy. She and I bonded very quickly. We were both a little lonely and homesick. Somehow, I got through registration, found all my classes, found the library, found the cafeteria, and made new friends. I was a genuine college student.

I left my home of 18 years; the security of having a large extended

Johnson Hall. The window of my dorm room is on the top left corner.

family close by; my high school friends; all the festive Sunday gatherings; my little sister, Carole; and a small town where I knew everyone. But, I was filled with anticipation and eager for the next chapter of my life to begin.

Charlie's girl left the farm.

Acknowledgments

A big thank you

- To my daughter, Deb, for giving me two books a number of years ago in which to record my memories.
- To my husband, Bob, for thinking my childhood memories were interesting and encouraging me to write more about my life on the farm and for all of his help with photos, editing, and keeping it fun.
- To my brothers, Duane and Norris, who were a wealth of information.
- To my sister, Carole, for her continual encouragement and helping fill in all of the blanks.
- To my sister-in-law, Norma, for her stories.
- To my friend, Rodger Wedgeworth, for his dedicated editing.
- To the Cambridge Museum for their assistance and cooperation.
- To the Arapahoe Museum for opening their doors just for me.

And to my Grandma Perdue for her journal.

References:

"A Century of Progress – 1874-1974," Cambridge Centennial Book

Nebraskastudies.org

Casde.unl.edu

Frontier County Historical Society Newsletter Summer 2017

Cambridge Clarion

U.S. Geological Survey

explainthatstuff.com

history.com

nsbma.org

Butler Memorial Library

Cambridge Pubic School

"Bluff-to-Bluff - The 1935 Republican Valley Flood" and "Bluff-to-Bluff Too - The 1935 Republican Valley Flood," by Marlene (Harvey) Wilmont

"The Hardship Trail – A Century of Unyielding Heritage," by Marlene (Harvey) Wilmont

"The 1935 Republican River Flood," by Joy Hayden

67855691R00112